D1361742

The Dictopedia

M-Z

by Pleasant T. Rowland

Tonia Lapham, Lorenca Consuelo Rosal,
and Alexander Humez, contributing writers

Developed by
Boston Educational Research Company

▲▼Addison-Wesley Publishing Company

Menlo Park, California • Reading, Massachusetts • London • Amsterdam • Don Mills, Ontario • Sydney

Acknowledgments

M page 7, Shirleyann Costigan. Page 13, T. Lapham. Pages 14 and 15 (left), L. Rosal. Page 15 (right), T. Lapham. Page 16, adaptation of "The Smallest Dragonboy" by Anne McCaffrey. From *Science Fiction Tales* edited by Roger Elwood. Copyright 1973 by Rand McNally & Co. Page 28, Shirleyann Costigan. Page 31, T. Lapham. Page 32, T. Lapham. Page 34, Janet Bosworth.

N page 36, from the Book *Toolchest* by Jan Adkins. Copyright©1973 by Jan Adkins. By permission of the publisher, Walker and Company. Page 38, T. Lapham. Page 39, "The Great Voice in the Sea," Shirleyann Costigan. Page 44, L. Rosal. Page 45, Candelaria Silva. Page 47, Shirleyann Costigan. Page 51, Shirleyann Costigan. Page 52, "Good Night," T. Lapham. Page 55, Shirleyann Costigan.

O page 60, A. Humez, based on an idea by Amy Whitney. Page 61, "Oasis," Janet Bosworth. Page 62, "Obblebumps," L. Rosal. Page 78, adapted from *The Survivors: Enduring Animals of North America,* © 1975 by Jack Denton Scott. Reprinted by permission of Harcourt Brace Jovanovich, Inc. British rights by permission of the author and Raines & Raines. Page 80 (left), adapted from *Arm in Arm* by Remy Charlip. Copyright © 1969 by Remy Charlip. Page 80 (right), from *Perplexing Puzzles and Tantalizing Teasers,* an adaptation of "Mother Hubbard's Cupboard," copyright 1969 by Martin Gardner. Reprinted by permission of Simon & Schuster, Childrens Book Division. Page 81, "The Case of the Black Onyx Cat," L. Rosal. Page 88, L. Rosal and A. Humez. Page 90 (left), from *Jokes, Puns and Riddles* by David Allen Clark. Copyright © 1968 by Doubleday & Company, Inc. Reprinted by permission of the publisher. Page 90 (right), text copyright © 1967 by Lilian Moore, from *I Feel the Same Way,* used by permission of Atheneum Publishers.

P page 91, Martha Green. Page 92 (left), A. Humez. Page 92 (right), L. Rosal. Page 93, adapted from *Victorian Inventions* by Leonard de Vries. Copyright © 1971 by Leonard de Vries. Reprinted by permission of John Murray (Publishers) Ltd. Page 99, from *Talking Words* by Ashok Davar, copyright © 1969 by Ashok Davar. Reprinted by permission of The Bobbs-Merrill Co., Inc. Page 100, A. Humez. Page 101, "Ping-Pong," from *Finding a Poem* by Eve Merriam. Reprinted by permission of Eve Merriam, c/o International Creative Management. Copyright © 1970 by Eve Merriam. Page 102, Martha Green. Page 105, "The Promise of Spring," L. Rosal. Page 113, "Period," "Comma," "Exclamation Point," "Question Mark," and "Apostrophe" all from *Words Words Words* by Mary O'Neill. Copyright © 1966 by Mary O'Neill. Reprinted by permission of Doubleday & Company, Inc. Page 116, L. Rosal.

Q page 117, from *Q's Are Weird O's* by Roy Doty. Copyright © 1975 by Roy Doty. Reprinted by permission of Doubleday & Company, Inc. Page 118, reproduced by permission of the publisher from *Contes Dramatiques,* ed. by Hills and Dondo, © 1960 by D. C. Heath and Company, Lexington, Massachusetts. Page 123, "The Quagga Is Dead," Shirleyann Costigan. Page 124, adapted from *Science Puzzlers* by Martin Gardner. Copyright © 1960 by Martin Gardner and Anthony Ravielli. By permission of The Viking Press. Page 125, "A Small Discovery" by James A. Emanuel. Reprinted by permission of the author. Page 131, "Quiet" from *The Malibu and Other Poems* by Myra Cohn Livingston (A Margaret K. McElderry Book). Copyright © 1972 by Myra Cohn Livingston. Used by permission of Atheneum Publishers. Page 133 (top), Candelaria Silva. Page 133 (bottom), from *26 Ways of Looking at a Black Man* by Raymond R. Patterson. Copyright © 1969 by Raymond R. Patterson. Page 134, adapted from *Agent K-13 the Super-Spy* by Robert L.

Teague. Copyright © 1974 by Robert L. Teague. Reprinted by permission of Doubleday & Company, Inc.

R page 143, "No Nonsense" by Scott Corbett. Reprinted by permission of Curtis Brown Ltd. Copyright © 1974 by Scott Corbett. Page 150 (top left), "Spring rain" from *Haiku* Vols. 1–4 by R. H. Blyth. Reprinted by permission of The Hokuseido Press, Tokyo. Page 150 (top right), "A summer shower…" from *A History of Haiku* Vol. 1 by R. H. Blyth. Reprinted by permission of The Hokuseido Press. Page 150 (bottom), translated by A. Humez and E. Goldfrank. Page 151 (left), A. Humez. Page 152, "Finders Keepers" by Bonnie Wasser. Copyright © 1977, *Highlights for Children, Inc.*, Columbus, Ohio. Page 159, A. Humez. Page 160, T. Lapham. Page 162, adapted from a story by Matt Brandis.

S page 168, from *Arm in Arm* by Remy Charlip. Copyright © 1969 by Remy Charlip. Page 170, A. Humez. Page 171, adapted from "My First Year at School, 1895" by Vera Gerken Kurtz, *Learning* (Magazine for Creative Teaching), February, 1976. Copyright © 1976 by Education Today Company, Inc. Page 177, L. Rosal. Page 178, adapted from "My Sister, the Snake, and I" by Yolanda Ferguson Stein. Copyright © 1976 by Yolanda Ferguson Stein. Page 184, from *Woody and Me*, by Mary Neville and Ronni Solbert. Copyright © 1966 by Mary Neville Woodrich and Ronni Solbert. Reprinted by permission of Pantheon Books, a Division of Random House, Inc. Page 185, L. Rosal and A. Humez. Page 186, adapted from *Sticks* by Oliver G. Selfridge. Pictures by John E. Johnson. Copyright © 1967 by Oliver G. Selfridge and John E. Johnson. Reprinted by permission of Houghton Mifflin Company. Page 193 (left), T. Lapham. Page 193 (right), "The Sun Is Stuck" by Myra Cohn Livingston. Copyright © 1969 by Myra Cohn Livingston. Reprinted by permission of McIntosh and Otis, Inc. Page 194, Martha Green.

T page 196, from *Sharpen Your Wits* by Gerard Mosler. Copyright© 1971 by Gerard Mosler. Reprinted by permission of Doubleday & Company, Inc. Page 197, from *Only the Moon and Me* by Richard J. Margolis. Copyright ©1969 by Richard J. Margolis. Reprinted by permission of J. B. Lippincott Company. Page 198, A. Humez. Page 200, adapted from *Ounce Dice Trice* by Alastair Reid, by permission of Little, Brown and Co. in association with *The Atlantic Monthly Press*. Copyright ©1958 by Alastair Reid and Ben Shahn. Page 203, L. Rosal.

Page 204, "Two Touching Toughies" from *The Hand Book* by Lassor Blumenthal. Copyright © 1976 by Lassor A. Blumenthal. Reprinted by permission of Doubleday & Company, Inc. Page 205, adapted from the book *Unnatural Resources: True Stories of American Treasure* by Dale M. Titler. Copyright © 1973 by Dale M. Titler. Published by Prentice-Hall, Inc., Englewood Cliffs, New Jersey. Page 210 (bottom), from *Riddles, Jokes and Other Funny Things* by Bill Gerler, John Norment, and Peter Pendragon. Copyright © 1975 by Western Publishing Company, Inc. Used by permission. Page 211, text adapted from *Kelly's Creek* by Doris Buchanan Smith. Copyright © 1975 by Doris Buchanan Smith. Reprinted by permission of Thomas Y. Crowell Company.

U page 224, A. Humez. Page 225, adapted from "Through the Window" by Naoshi Koriyama. Reprinted by permission from The Christian Science Monitor. © 1955 The Christian Science Publishing Society. All rights reserved. Page 226, copyright 1949 by Marion Holland. Reprinted from *Billy Had a System*, by Marion Holland. Adapted by permission of Alfred A. Knopf, Inc. Page 235 (right), from *I'm Like Me* by Siv Widerberg. © 1971 Siv Widerberg. Translation © 1973 by Verne Moberg. Reprinted by permission of The Feminist Press, Box 334, Old Westbury, N.Y. 11568. Page 236, "Unicorn," Janet Bosworth. Page 240, adapted from *Tripping in America* by Bill Thomas. Copyright 1974 by the author. Reprinted with the permission of the publisher, Chilton Book Co., Radnor, Pennsylvania. Page 244, adapted from *Perplexing Puzzles and Tantalizing Teasers*. Copyright © 1969 by Martin Gardner. Reprinted by permission of Simon & Schuster, a Division of Gulf & Western Corporation. Page 245, adapted from *A Walk on an Iceberg* by Mary Ellen Chase. Text copyright © 1966 by Mary Ellen Chase. Used by permission of Grosset & Dunlap, Inc. Page 250, "Ups and Downs," A. Humez.

V page 252, from "Ruins Under the Stars" by Galway Kinnell in *Flower Herding on Mount Monadnock*. © 1964 by Galway Kinnell. Reprinted by permission of Houghton Mifflin Company. Page 253, from *Puzzles, Stunts, Brain Teasers and Tricks* from "Tell Me Why" by Arkady Leokum. Copyright © 1969 by Arkady Leokum. Page 254, T. Lapham. Page 257, L. Rosal, from a story by Janet Bosworth. Page 260, T. Lapham and L. Rosal. Page 264, adapted from *Tales of a Fourth Grade Nothing* by Judy Blume.

(Acknowledgments continued on page 335.)

3

Table of Contents

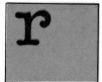

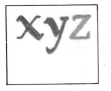

6

make-believe

Imagine a magical castle
In a wonderful, magical land,
With a prince and a princess so little,
They could dance in the palm of your hand.
And imagine that you are invited
To go to a glittering ball
In honor of some royal princess,
But everything there is so small,
You can only peep in through the window.
(Your foot wouldn't fit through the door.)
But at least you can hear all the music
And watch as the dancers explore
That beautiful, magical castle,
In that wonderful, magical land,
With a prince and a princess so little,
They could dance in the palm of your hand.

You enter the great hall. Its shiny floor is like a mirror. A winding golden staircase leads upstairs. Everyone looks up, waiting for the prince and princess to come down.

The dining hall is ready for a feast. The table is set with golden goblets and plates. Twinkling candles light this splendid room.

Meanwhile, in his room upstairs, the handsome prince has put down his sword to get ready for the royal dance. His golden shoes lie next to his bed.

On the other side of the castle, the young princess dresses for her very first dance. She sits on the edge of her golden bed, which looks like a fairy boat covered with a great, golden cobweb. The princess puts on her tiny glass slippers and is ready to join the prince.

9

Magical? Yes. Make-believe? No, not quite. The castle you just visited is real. And it's just as beautiful as any make-believe castle could be. But it is a miniature castle. Everything about it is very small. A woman named Colleen Moore spent her life collecting small furniture, books, dishes, and flowers for this magical castle. When it was finished, she gave it to a city museum for everyone to look at and enjoy. Colleen Moore's granddaughter, who is twelve years old, shows the true size of the castle.

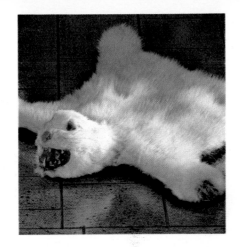

The piano is so small that it can easily sit on a sheet of music.

Ordinary books show how small the bookcase in the castle really is.

In the prince's bedroom is a bear rug. Its teeth came from a mouse.

In the kitchen, pans and kettles hang on the wall. The oven looks ready to use. Dishes are set out to be filled. But a real onion in this room is as high as the table itself!

marsh

A marsh is a low, flat, grassy place that is covered with water part of the time. If a marsh is near the ocean and has salty water flowing in and out, it is called a saltwater marsh.

Salt Marsh

The marsh grass
Shaking, swaying
In the ocean's breeze.

The flowing tide
Swimming, sweeping
Across the sun-swept marsh.

Marsh dwellers
Swooping, splashing
In the secret shallow.

The flowing tide
Swimming, sweeping
Back to its ocean home.

13

Herrings

Silvery herrings swim
Beneath clouds
Of hungry gulls.

Raccoon

Raccoon
Builds a nest of
Stalks and grass.

Raccoon
Rests on its
Half-floating bed.

Raccoon
Waits for the tide
To leave supper!

Periwinkle

Periwinkle
Twinkling
 on a
Wrinkling
Blade of grass.

14

Bittern's Love Song

A little bird inflates his neck
Like a birthday balloon,
Shows a long-hidden white feather
Beneath his wings,
Bends his head forward and cries,
Thump! Thump! Thunder-Pumper!

Cattails

Where cattails grow
It's hard to go—
At least for me.

The marshy land
Part mud, part sand—
Too wet for me.

On stalks so tall
The blackbirds call—
But not for me.

I stand beside
The creeping tide—
And smell the sea.

15

mind reader

A mind reader is someone who knows what someone else is thinking without being told.

Keevan lengthened his stride as far as his legs would stretch, but he just couldn't keep up with the others. He knew he would be teased again for being the smallest dragonboy. He would arrive last and maybe get a frown from F'nor, the dragonrider in charge of the boys.

A good record was very important now. It was nearly hatching time, when the baby dragons would crack their shells and choose their companions for life. To be chosen—to be a dragonrider! To be the friend of a winged beast with jewel eyes! To hear each other's thoughts! To fly on the dragon's back over the lands of Pern!

Keevan wondered what was wrong with being small. People were always calling him "baby" and saying he was "too small" or "too young." He worked twice as hard as any other boy his age

to prove himself. And if he couldn't beat anyone in a wrestling match, he could outrun everyone in a race.

"Maybe if you run fast enough," Beterli had jeered once, "you can catch a dragon. That's the only way you'll make a dragonrider." Beterli was the oldest and biggest of the boys, and he always made fun of Keevan.

"Wait and see, Beterli," Keevan had said. "No one knows what wins a dragon."

Mende, Keevan's foster mother, told him, "I believe that dragons see into a person's heart. If they find goodness, honesty, patience, courage—that's what dragons look for."

As Keevan came to the Hatching Grounds, F'nor was already speaking. His face was serious.

"As we all know," F'nor said, "there are only forty dragon eggs. There are seventy-two candidates. Some of you will be disappointed on hatching day. That doesn't mean you'll never be a dragonrider. It just means that *the* dragon for you hasn't been born. It's no disgrace to be left behind for a hatching or two. Or more."

Keevan was sure F'nor looked at Beterli, who'd been at eight hatchings already. Keevan tried to squinch down so F'nor wouldn't see him. If Keevan's birthday had been one day later, he would have been too young to be a candidate. He was the most likely to be left without a dragon.

"I don't know why you're allowed at this hatching, Keevan. There are enough candidates without a baby," Beterli said.

"I'm of age," Keevan answered.

"Yah! You can't even see over an egg," Beterli said with a sneer.

"You'd better make sure a dragon sees *you* this time, Beterli. You're almost too old, aren't you?"

Beterli raised his fist. Keevan stood still. Just then, F'nor called the boys together for their evening chores.

During dinner, Keevan heard the dragonriders talking. There were so many boys and so few eggs. Some riders said the youngest candidates should wait till next year. Keevan left the hall and sat in the kitchen, trying not to cry.

"Whatever is the matter with you?" Mende asked when she saw him.

"They're going to keep me from this hatching. You heard them talking. They're going to drop the babies from the hatching."

Mende touched his arm gently. "I've heard the same nonsense before every hatching. But nothing is ever changed. Now bring in some coal. If the eggs do hatch today, we'll need fires for the feast. Don't worry. All my foster sons make dragonriders."

Keevan reached the coal pile just as Beterli arrived, too.

"Heard the news, baby?" asked Beterli. He was grinning from ear to ear.

"Are the eggs cracking?" Keevan nearly dropped his coal shovel.

"Naw! Guess again!" Beterli seemed very pleased with himself.

With a sinking heart, Keevan knew what the news must be. The youngest candidates must have been dropped out.

"Come on! Guess, baby!"

"I've no time for guessing games," Keevan managed to say. He began to shovel coal into his cart as fast as he could.

"I said—Guess!" Beterli grabbed the shovel and pulled it from Keevan's hands. "Guess!"

"Give me back the shovel, Beterli." Keevan straightened up. From somewhere, other boys appeared.

Keevan tried to pull his shovel away from Beterli. The bigger boy pulled back, but Keevan held on. Suddenly, Beterli rammed the handle into Keevan's chest, knocking him over. Keevan felt a sharp pain in his right leg, then blackness.

When he woke, he was tucked into his bed. His leg was in splints. He could hear voices—Mende and Lessa, the head woman of the dragonriders. He remembered Beterli and the quarrel. . . . It must be serious, to bring Lessa here.

Not only did she ride the golden queen dragon; she could hear the thoughts of *all* the dragons. Other riders could only hear their own dragons. And now Lessa, the queenrider, was asking him about Beterli.

"What happened at the coal pile?" she asked him.

"'Beterli took the shovel. I hadn't finished with it," Keevan answered.

"There's more than one shovel. What did he *say* to you?" Lessa asked.

"That . . . that . . . there had been changes," Keevan said.

"What did he say, exactly?" Lessa demanded impatiently.

"He said for me to guess the news." Keevan felt like a fool.

"Remember all the talk at supper last night, Lessa," said Mende. "Of course Keevan thought he'd been dropped."

"Don't worry, Keevan," Lessa said. "You'll have other hatchings. Beterli will not. There are certain rules about playing fair. Beterli will never make a dragonrider." Lessa left the room.

"Am I still a candidate?" Keevan asked Mende.

"Well, you are and you aren't," she said, leaving. "You just rest."

Alone, Keevan lay there worrying. Where were the other boys? Something was wrong. Only he didn't know what.

Then he heard the humming. It started low, almost too low to be heard. Then the hum grew. Two thoughts burst suddenly in Keevan's sleepy mind: The only white candidate's robe still on the hook was his. And dragons hummed

23

when the eggs were being hatched! Hatching! And he was flat in bed with a broken leg.

No one had said he couldn't go to the hatching. "You are and you aren't" were Mende's exact words.

Keevan sat up and touched the splinted leg. He swung himself carefully to the side of the bed. Slowly he stood up. The room seemed to spin around him. He jerked his white robe from the hook. Now he needed something to lean on. And he knew there were some long sticks on the lower floor.

Gritting his teeth and blinking back tears, Keevan scrambled down the ramp. It wasn't far to the sticks, but it seemed an age before he had one in his hand.

Then the humming stopped!

Keevan cried out and tried to hurry. The only sounds were his ragged breathing and the thump of his stick on the hard ground. Twice he fell and pulled himself up on the stick.

He heard a cheer! An egg had cracked, and the dragon had chosen its rider. Another cheer! If he didn't get there in moments, there would be no baby dragons left.

Then he was at the Hatching Grounds, the sand hot on his bare feet. No one saw him come in. And he could see nothing but the crowd. More cheers. Another boy had been chosen. Now there was a gap, and Keevan could see the eggs. There didn't seem to be any left uncracked.

Suddenly he wished he had stayed away, had stayed in bed. Everyone would see his failure. He turned and tried to reach the shadowy walls of the Hatching Grounds. He mustn't be seen.

He didn't notice when the crowd began to move in his direction. He tripped and fell sobbing on the warm sand. He didn't hear all the excited whispers.

"I've never seen anything like it," someone was saying. "Only thirty-nine riders chosen. And one dragon trying to leave the Hatching Grounds without choosing a rider."

Then Keevan heard voices nearing him. He hid his face in the sand. How everyone would tease him!

DON'T WORRY! PLEASE DON'T WORRY. He heard the thought, but it was not his thought!

Someone kicked sand over Keevan and pushed him roughly.

"Go away. Just leave me alone," Keevan cried.

26

WHY? There was no voice, but the question was there in his mind.

Keevan looked up and stared into the glowing eyes of a small dragon. His wings were wet. The tips drooped on the sand. And he wobbled on unsteady legs.

WHY? asked the dragon again. DON'T YOU LIKE ME? His eyes were frightened, and his tone was sad. Keevan staggered forward and threw his arms around the dragon's neck. Keevan patted the dragon and opened its wings to dry them. Over and over in his mind, he told the dragon, "You are the most wonderful dragon on all Pern."

"What's his name, K'van?" asked Lessa. She smiled at the new dragon-rider. And K'van smiled back. K'van. His new, shorter name meant he was really a dragonrider.

MY NAME IS HEATH, thought the dragon. AND I'M HUNGRY!

"Dragons are always hungry," laughed Lessa, who could hear all the dragons. "Here, let someone help you. You can hardly stand, much less help your dragon."

K'van pulled himself up on his stick. "We'll be just fine, thank you." He put his arm around Heath's neck. The smallest dragonboy and the dragon who would not choose anyone else walked out together.

mold

very tiny plants that grow in groups

Mold is so tiny that you usually can't see it. But if you leave something like a piece of bread or an orange or an old sneaker in a dark, warm, damp place, you'll soon see mold begin to grow. Here's how you can grow your own Mighty Mold.

1. Get a piece of bread. To help your mold start growing, get your bread a little dirty. Wipe it on the floor or windowsill.

2. Sprinkle some water on your bread. Don't give it a bath—your mold doesn't like to swim.

Put your bread into a
and cover it tightly.
ve your mold a hiding
ce. Keep the jar in a
rm, dark spot like a
set.

4. Look at your bread
each day. When the mold
begins to grow, give it a
name. Call it Woolly
Willy or Moldy Goldie or
Fungusamungus—
something catchy like
that. Say things like
"Come on, Fungus-
amungus!" or "Wiggle
your whiskers, Willy!"
You might even put your
mold's name on the jar.
That will make the mold
feel important.

5. The mold on your
bread will appreciate all
this attention and care.
By the end of the week,
you should have some
healthy mold.

6. If you want to get to
know your mold better,
you can look at it under
a magnifying glass.
It won't mind. It will
think that it's on TV.

month

Knuckle Calendar

There are 12 months in a year. The long months have 31 days. The short months have 30 days, except February, which has 28. It is important to know which are the long months and which are the short months if you are counting the days until your birthday or summer vacation.

The Knuckle Calendar is a very simple way of telling which months are long and which months are short. Make a fist with your left hand. With a finger of your right hand, touch the knuckle mountains and the valleys between the knuckles. As you do this, name the months. All the long months will be on the knuckle mountains. All the short months will fall into the little valleys.

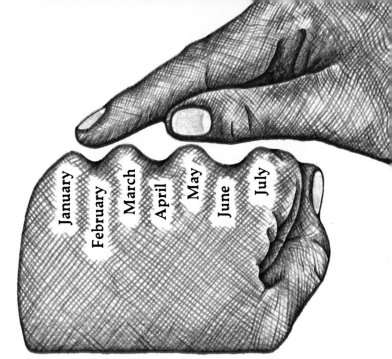

January February March April May June July

(Now go back to the first knuckle.)

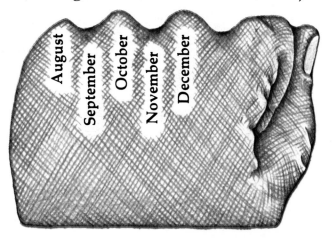

August September October November December

mosquito

All the mighty mosquitoes *buzz* zing *buzz* zing went out to look for dinner. yum yum

"A tasty leg chomp chomp or a juicy arm **slurp slurp** sounds like a good dinner," yum yum said the mighty mosquitoes, *buzz* zing and off they flew.

Now it happened that the juicy arm **slurp slurp** and the tasty leg chomp chomp that the mighty mosquitoes *buzz* zing chose for dinner yum yum belonged to Miniver Musselmouth. oh me oh my

When Miniver Musselmouth oh me oh my saw who had come for dinner yum yum she said, "The mighty mosquitoes *buzz* zing are not going to munch my juicy arm **slurp slurp** or tasty leg. chomp chomp Mighty mosquitoes *buzz* zing that mess around with Miniver Musselmouth oh me oh my will meet with a messy misfortune!" **splat!**

31

mountain

If you want to camp in the mountains, you have to plan carefully.

1. Everything you need will be carried on your back, so make sure you have a comfortable backpack. A lightweight tent can be rolled up for carrying.

2. You will sleep comfortably in a lightweight sleeping bag—especially if there is a pad underneath you.

3. Take a toothbrush and toothpaste, some soap, some toilet paper, and a small towel.

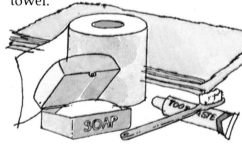

4. Bring a flashlight with extra batteries. Always carry a first-aid kit. It also helps to have a good knife and a big handkerchief.

32

5. Be ready for all kinds of weather. Pack a windbreaker or sweater, a warm hat, and extra socks.

6. You will need at least one pot with a lid. (Sometimes two pots fit together, so that one is a lid for the other.) Also pack a spoon, a fork, and a cup.

7. A small kerosene camp stove is important. Keep it in a metal case for safety.

8. Most of the food you will need can be found in supermarkets. Buy dried, instant, or quick-cooking foods.

9. If there is a little extra space, take along a camera and a book about plants or animals.

33

A man climbed to the
mountaintop.
Then into the valley
he cried,
"What a brave man,
what a strong man,
what a wise man
am I!"

The listening valley
echoed,
"Am I . . . am I . . . am I . . . ?

N

The letter N began as a hieroglyph
that looked like a snake.

First it straightened out.   Next it squiggled up.   Then it flopped over.

And at last it looked like this and this and this

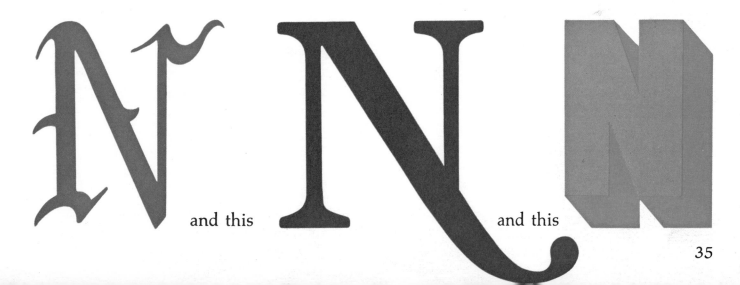

and this   and this

nail

Nails are brave. Heavy hammers beat on their heads, but they never complain. And nails never show off, even though they have a right to. Think of what nails do. They hold together pieces of wood and bricks and cement. They keep roofs from flying off houses. Nails make floors solid under your feet. Nails hold down carpets and keep chairs together. In fact, there isn't much that nails can't hold together.

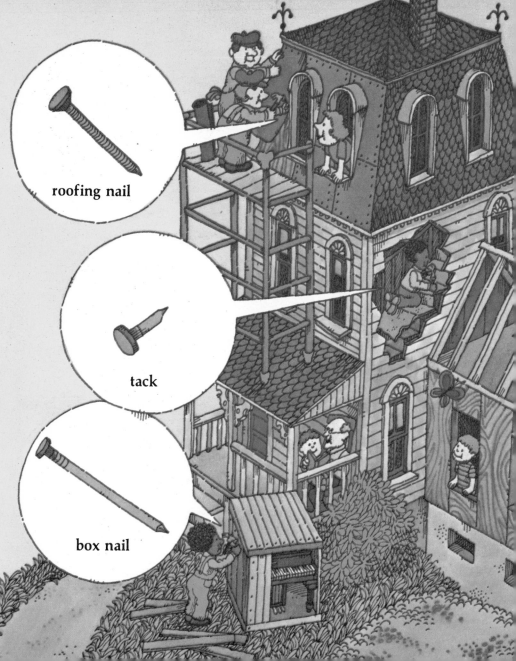

roofing nail

tack

box nail

common nail

finish nail

masonry nail

There are many different kinds of nails. Each kind is used for a different job.

Common nails are used for constructing buildings. Their wide, flat heads are easy to hit, so a building can go up quickly.

Box nails are thinner than common nails. They are used for big wooden boxes and crates, which do not need the stronger construction nails.

Finish nails are thin and have no heads. After they have been hammered into the wood, they can hardly be seen.

Roofing nails are short and thick. They are used to attach tarpaper to roofs.

Tacks are short and have sharp, sharp points. They are used for carpets and other heavy material.

Masonry nails are extra hard. They can be hammered into brick and cement without bending.

37

name

Everyone in this picture is named Terry. If you want to talk about *one* of them, how do you explain which one you mean?

- Which one is Terry Fisher?
- One Terry makes shoes. What is that Terry called?
- Where does Terry Forest live?
- Why is the Terry with black hair called Terry Baker?
- Which Terrys have these last names? Fiddler, Wheeler, Potts

Your last name probably started the same way. In almost all languages, last names came from the places where people lived, or what they did for a living, or what they looked like. Where does your last name come from?

nautical

having something to do with ships or sailors

The Great Voice in the Sea

Part One: Cubbins Goes to Sea

On a cold day in February, 1842, Cubbins MacNabb signed aboard ship for the first time. It was a whaling ship named *The Trumpet*, and it was about to leave on a three-year trip. Cubbins would be the ship's boy. He would work for the captain, the cook, and the other ship's officers. He would make very little money. But he would learn about the sea and ships and sailors. Most of all, he would learn about whaling.

Cubbins smiled as the captain welcomed him aboard. He felt very grown up to have this job, for whaling was important work. The whale fat, called blubber, was used to make whale oil. Whale oil was burned to light lamps. In those days

everyone used oil lamps, for there were no electric lights in 1842. So Cubbins was ready to go to work, and work he did.

Cubbins cleaned the cabins below deck, where the sailors slept, and he cleaned the galley, where they ate. But when the men on the ship killed a whale, he had to throw down his mop and help the rest of the crew. Nearly everyone on the ship did whale work when a whale was caught.

Every time a whale was killed, *The Trumpet* turned into a factory at sea. First the dead whale was tied to the side of the ship. Then the men cut away long strips of blubber from the whale's body. The blubber was sliced into smaller pieces and tossed into big cooking pots to boil. From the boiled blubber came the precious oil. After the oil cooled, it was poured into wooden barrels and stored in the belly of the ship.

Everyone worked day and night until the job

was done. The fires under the cooking pots sent up a rotten stink and greasy smoke. The decks became slippery with oily ooze. Everyone's clothes stank from grease. It was the smelliest, messiest job Cubbins had ever known. And he hated it.

But it wasn't just the messy work that Cubbins hated. Something else bothered him, too. One clear April day he went up on deck to speak to his friend Angus about it. Angus, the ship's helmsman, was at the wheel, steering the ship.

He smiled when he saw Cubbins and let the boy take the wheel.

"Angus," Cubbins said after a little while, "tell me about the whales. What kind of creatures are they, really?"

"Gentle creatures," answered the helmsman. "They are playful and kind to each other—almost human. Some people think that whales talk to each other, the way we do. I don't know about that. Yet once I heard a strange, deep voice in the

41

sea. Others have heard it, too. Perhaps it was the whales calling to each other—or calling to us. I don't know."

"But they are so big and powerful," said Cubbins. "Aren't they dangerous?"

"They can be dangerous, of course," Angus answered, "but only when they are attacked. How would you like to be stabbed with a harpoon?"

Cubbins didn't answer. He wondered why Angus sailed on a whaling ship if he liked the whales so much. Cubbins was just about to ask when suddenly he heard a cry.

"Whales! Whales! Whales ahead!"

Cubbins's heart jumped and then fell into the pit of his stomach. On the last chase, a whale had smashed one of the small boats to smithereens. Three of the crew had drowned. But Cubbins knew he couldn't hide below deck. The captain expected him to stay.

Cubbins watched the crew row their small boats out to the whales. One boat rowed up close

to one of the larger whales. Then the harpooner threw a harpoon deep into its back. Again and again the men stabbed the thrashing whale with harpoons. The struggle lasted for hours. The water turned red with blood.

Sometimes in the past a wounded whale had gotten away. But on this day, the whale finally lost. It grew weak and rolled over on its back. The harpooner stabbed it again. Blood spurted into the air. The whale was dead.

Cubbins turned away. He felt sick. Suddenly he hated everything about his new life. He hated the ship, the sailors, and the sea. He even hated the whales.

"Never again," he said to himself. "When this trip is over, I will never again go to sea." And he really believed what he said, until one strange night in October when everything changed.

To be continued.

need

Neil kneads bread.

Neil needs bread.

Neil needs help.

Neil kneads "help."

44

never mind

My momma's mad at me. She asked me to find her brown thread. I can't find it.

I look on her dresser, in her desk, in her top drawer, and in the sewing-machine stand. I see black, red, green, and orange thread, but no brown.

This is the third time she's sent me back upstairs to look.

I can still hear her saying, "If I go up there and find it, you're going to be in trouble. It's probably right in front of your nose."

"I can't find it, Momma. I looked real hard," I said.

"Never mind. I'll find it myself," she said.

"But—" I said.

45

"Never mind, Richard," she said.

"I'll look again," I said.

"No, Richard. I said—Never mind. If you would pay more attention to things...."

I sit down, read my book, and try to breathe very quietly so she won't notice me and get madder. I peek over at her to see what she's doing. She's sewing my pants with brown thread!

"Where'd you find the brown thread, Momma?" I ask.

"Never mind. At least *I* found it," she says.

She looks embarrassed. I'll bet she was sitting on it, like the last time we couldn't find something.

"What are you laughing about, child?"

"Never mind, Momma."

46

nevermore

never again

The Great Voice in the Sea

Part Two: October Storm

October brought bad weather. At first it was clear and windy, and *The Trumpet* had good sailing. But then came a calm; there was no wind at all—not a breeze, not a breath. The ship moved slowly, with no wind to fill its sails. Day after day Cubbins MacNabb watched the gray skies and waited for rain.

Finally it came—not just rain, but a hurricane. Howling winds and stabbing rains battered the ship. Giant waves scooped it up and spilled it down like a tiny toy.

No one stood at the ship's helm, for no one dared to go on deck. Below deck, Angus tried to hold *The Trumpet* on course. But the wind was

stronger than he was. So for three days the ship tossed without direction.

The sailors worked for their lives. They pumped water out of the leaking ship and made constant repairs. Meanwhile, Angus and the captain studied their maps to figure out where the storm was taking them.

But Cubbins stayed in his narrow cabin. The wild waves made him seasick. He clung to his bunk to keep from banging into the walls. He cried. He called for his mother. He thought he was going to die.

"This is the end of me," said Cubbins to himself.

But it was not the end. In time the wind began to die down, and the rain began to fall more gently. Soon Cubbins felt only the steady rocking of the ship. And at last he fell asleep.

When he woke up, the storm was over. Filled with new hope, he scrambled to join the rest of

the crew. But when he reached the deck, his heart sank.

Bright moonlight lit up the night. *The Trumpet* was in bad shape. Hatch covers were torn away. A mast was broken, and most of the sails hung in tatters. Equipment was missing. One of the sailors was missing, too, someone told him. No one seemed to know how or when it had happened.

And there was other trouble. The storm had driven *The Trumpet* into waters filled with reefs. These ridges of sharp shells grew from the ocean bottom and could tear a ship apart.

The frightened sailors were very tired, but they could not rest. They had to get *The Trumpet* out of the dangerous waters. Some of the crew were hanging lanterns over the side of the ship. Others were shouting directions to Angus so that he could steer the ship safely through the maze of reefs.

Cubbins moved near Angus.

"We're in trouble," Angus said to the captain. "The storm has brought us close to a good port. But these waters are filled with reefs, and the moon will soon set. We won't be able to see our way."

Cubbins groaned.

Now he understood why the sailors were hanging lanterns on the sides of the ship. Once the moon set, it would be difficult to see the dangerous reefs. The lanterns would give some light, but not much. *The Trumpet* was in trouble. One scrape against a reef and it would surely sink.

"Life at sea is just one long misery," said Cubbins. "Nevermore. Never, nevermore will I return to the sea. Never, if I get home alive."

To be continued.

no

You know when
No . . .
Is on its way,
That little word
So hard to say.
First comes
Maybe . . .
Then
Well, I don't know . . .
Then
We'll see . . .
Then
I don't think so . . .
And then
You know what's coming next.
You know it's
No.

51

noise

I always lie
   in bed at night
   and listen . . .

What's that I hear?
   Will that noise bite?
   I'll listen . . .

I sit up straight
   with sheet held tight
   and listen . . .

Where is that noise?
It's not in sight.
I'll listen . . .

I leap from bed,
turn on the light,
and listen . . .

Then feeling brave,
off goes the light;
I'll listen . . .

What's that I hear?
Will that noise bite?
I'll listen . . .

53

I sit up straight
with sheet held tight
and listen . . .

Where is that noise?
It's not in sight.
I'll listen . . .

SWish swush swish swush
clinkity clinkity clinkity
Woo-hoo Woo-hoo

I've had enough.
I shout **GOOD NIGHT**

and listen . . .

ZZZZZZZZ Z Z Z Z Z ZZ

54

November

the eleventh month of the year

The Great Voice in the Sea

Part Three: November Morning

The last October moon set, and the water turned inky black. *The Trumpet* rocked gently, its lanterns swinging back and forth. The lights made the ship look very jolly, but the crew was frightened. *The Trumpet* was struggling to stay afloat. Dangerous reefs were all around. Angus, the helmsman, could not see which way to turn. The crew stood and searched the water. Every few minutes someone would shout a warning.

"Reef to the starboard side!"

"Reef dead ahead!"

Then Angus would turn the wheel hard. *The Trumpet* would groan miserably as it changed course.

Cubbins also stood at the rail. His eyes burned from searching the black water. He thought the night would never end.

Then, with a sudden, heart-stopping shock, great voice sounded beneath the ship. It thrummed. It rumbled up through the ship and broke into the night air. Everyone froze.

"What was that?" asked the captain.

Then it came again, a thrumming wave of sound, like mighty organ music. Cubbins's arms turned all goosebumpy. Angus stood still and listened hard.

"It's coming from the southwest," Angus said. "It seems to be moving toward safe waters."

"But what *is* it?" asked the captain.

"I don't know," answered Angus. "But I think it wants us to follow."

"Angus, you're crazy," said the captain.

But again the voice called. Angus spun the helm, and like a trusting dog, *The Trumpet* followed the strange voice.

The sailors continued to watch for reefs. But, amazingly, the reefs seemed to have disappeared. The voice was leading them through a clear path in the water.

Suddenly, one hour before dawn, the voice stopped.

Everyone stood still and listened to the silence. Somehow they knew the danger was over.

Most of the crew went below. But Cubbins stayed on deck with Angus and waited for the sunrise. For a long time neither one spoke.

Finally, Cubbins dared to ask, "What was it, Angus?"

"A whale," he answered. "I'm sure it was a whale."

Cubbins nodded. "Yes," he said to himself.

In the distance they could see the lights of a port town. Before going below, the captain ran up a flag signaling for help. In the morning someone would see it and send a boat to lead them safely into port.

It would be months before *The Trumpet* could sail again. It needed many repairs. Cubbins would have to find work on another ship—but not on a whaler. Not after last night. The great voice of a whale had brought him and *The Trumpet* safely to port. Cubbins knew he could never watch a whale chase again.

"No, not a whaler," he thought. "I'll sign aboard a fast merchant ship." Merchant ships sailed all over the world, picking up tea and silk and other valuable cargo. What an exciting life that would be!

Cubbins was surprised at himself. Just a few hours before, he had hated the sea. He had said that he would never go to sea again. Now everything had changed.

"Why?" he wondered.

Angus saw the change on the boy's face.

"Well, Cubbins," said Angus, "you have been through storms and reefs. You have seen the sea at its very worst, and you are still alive to talk

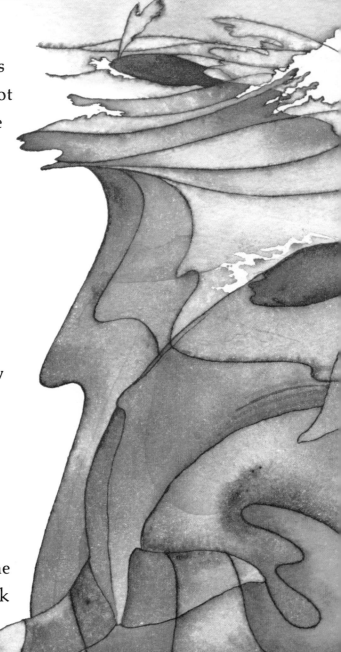

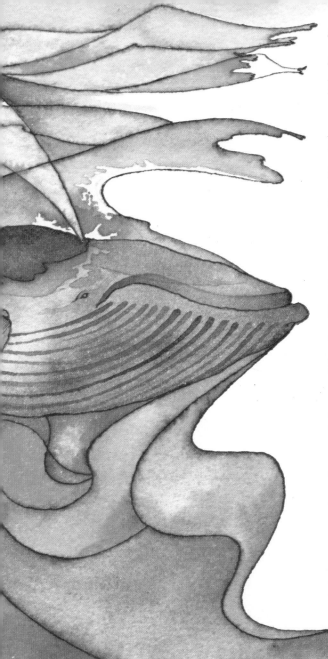

about it. Believe me, Cubbins, you will never be as frightened or as unhappy as you were before last night. You are a real sailor now."

Cubbins smiled. He did feel like a real sailor. But Angus was only partly right. There was something more—something that made all the difference. Cubbins had heard the great voice in the sea. It was as if the voice had been calling to him alone, telling him to follow and not to be afraid. That was why he felt so different. And that was why he could never work on another whaler. There was a tie of friendship between the boy and the great whales that would last forever.

"Angus," he said at last, "how did the whale know we needed help?"

"I don't know," answered his friend. "Perhaps it thought *The Trumpet* was a lost whale."

This made Cubbins laugh. And as he laughed, the sun began to rise on a new November morning.

Riddle:
Which letter is shaped
just like a pizza with its
middle missing? It's nearly the
sixteenth letter in the alphabet,
but it isn't quite. This letter can be
made by just drawing a circle. But
here's the real riddle: Why is this
riddle truly different? Because
every letter except the
mystery letter appears
in it.

Oasis
A COOL
refreshing
GREENNESS
IN THE SCORCHED
BROWN FACE
OF THE DESERT

obblebump

a large, orange vegetable that grows on vines

Cast of Characters

Jester	Elise, an obblebump grower
King of Zipp	First Soldier of Zipp
Prince Pump of Zipp	Second Soldier of Zipp
King of May	First Soldier of May
Princess Kin of May	Second Soldier of May

Act I

The two cities, Zipp and May, are at war. On one side of the stage is the King of Zipp's throne room. On the other side of the stage is the King of May's throne room. The Jester stands in the center. Make-believe arrows are being shot from one side of the stage to the other. The Jester keeps ducking the arrows while speaking.

Jester: Welcome, welcome to our play,
Where far ago and long away
The people fought
'Most every day.

Huge cannonballs and arrows, too,
Rocks and spears
Flew and flew
From Zipp to May
And back again.

The sound of war
Made Prince Pump
Of Zipp City
Shiver and jump.

(The Jester sits down at the front of the stage and watches. The King of Zipp looks very fierce. He is reading a battle map. His son, Prince Pump, looks unhappy.)

Prince Pump: I say, Father, why are we fighting the City of May?

King of Zipp: Questions, questions. Nothing but questions. Why don't you go shoot off a cannon or something?

Prince Pump: But, Father—

King of Zipp: I said, young man, go do something useful. Why not make yourself a crossbow? Just leave me alone. Can't you tell I'm busy with this war?

(Prince Pump and his father move off the stage. The Jester stands and steps to the center.)

Jester: Meanwhile in May,
Princess Kin began
To ask her father
Of the war in the land.

(The Jester sits down. The King of May and Princess Kin move forward and begin to speak. The King looks very fierce and is reading a battle map. The Princess looks unhappy.)

Princess Kin: Sorry to bother you, sir, but—

King of May: Bother? Bother? I'll tell you who's a bother. You! That's who. Now go make yourself a slingshot or something. And leave me alone. Can't you see I have a war to run?

65

Act II

Prince Pump and Princess Kin each go to the forest and look for wood. Elise, an obblebump grower, is also walking in the forest. The Jester stands alone in the middle of the stage.

Jester: So the Prince of Zipp
Went looking for wood
To make a crossbow
As best he could.

And the Princess of May
Went looking for wood
To make a slingshot
As best she could.

(The Jester sits down and waits for the prince and princess. Prince Pump enters, looking around for wood. Princess Kin comes on stage and looks at Prince Pump with surprise.)

Princess Kin: *entering* Oh, hello there. You're a Zipper, aren't you?

Prince Pump: No. I'm a prince.

Princess Kin: I know that, silly. I mean you're from the city of Zipp.

Prince Pump: *bowing* Yes, yes, of course I am. I'm Prince Pump of Zipp.

Princess Kin: *curtsying* How do you do? I'm Princess Kin of May.

Prince Pump: Pleased to meet you.

Princess Kin: Pleased? You're not supposed to be pleased.

Prince Pump: I'm not?

Princess Kin: No. You're supposed to be mad, nasty, and wild with anger. After all, I'm your enemy.

Prince Pump:	Oh, yes. I forgot. Tell me, why are you my enemy?
Princess Kin:	I don't know why. But our cities have been at war with each other for years. And since you are the Prince of Zipp and I am the Princess of May, then we should fight.
Prince Pump:	Well, I don't want to fight. Do you?
Princess Kin:	No.
Prince Pump:	That's good. Except I don't know what else to do. Maybe we should take a walk.
Princess Kin:	A walk would be a lot better than fighting.
Prince Pump: *tripping over something*	Oops! What are these big orange things all over the ground?
Elise: *entering*	Obblebumps. They grow all over this place. My mother and I pick them.
Princess Kin:	Obblebumps?

Elise:	Yes, obblebumps. You know, for obblebump pie.
Prince Pump:	Mmmmm. You don't say.
Elise:	Yes, I do say.
Princess Kin:	Wait a minute. Who are you, anyway? And how do you know so much about umblepumps—no, no. That's not right. Um, bamblebumps—no . . . um . . .
Elise:	Obblebumps. My name is Elise, and I live in the forest with my mother. We grow obblebumps.
Prince Pump:	You don't say.
Elise:	Yes, I do say.
Princess Kin:	Oh, please! Let's not start that again.
Elise:	Listen. Instead of fighting, why don't you grow obblebumps, too? Here are some seeds to plant in your gardens.
Prince Pump:	That's awfully kind of you.
Princess Kin:	We'll plant them everywhere.

Act III

Prince Pump and Princess Kin go home and plant obble-
bumps, as Elise suggested. Soon obblebumps cover both
towns. On one side of the stage are the soldiers of Zipp.
On the other side are the soldiers of May. The Jester
stands in the center of the stage between the two towns.

Jester: So the prince and princess
Hurried back home.
Each planted obblebumps
Of his or her own.

They watered and weeded
And waited until
Obblebumps sprouted
All over the hills.

Now the King of Zipp
Could not understand
Why obblebumps grew
All over his land.

(The Jester sits down, and the two soldiers of Zipp begin to speak.)

First Soldier: Hurry up. Get rid of these things. The King is coming to inspect the army!

Second Soldier: I'm trying, but they're everywhere.

King of Zipp: *entering and tripping over an obblebump* This is ridiculous! How can we fight a war when our cannons are covered with vines and these orange whatzamajiggles? Where is that noodle-head son of mine? I bet he knows something about this!

Prince Pump: Let me explain, Father. You see, I was out in the forest, under *your* orders, when whom should I meet . . .

(The King of Zipp, Prince Pump, and the soldiers go off the stage. The Jester steps forward.)

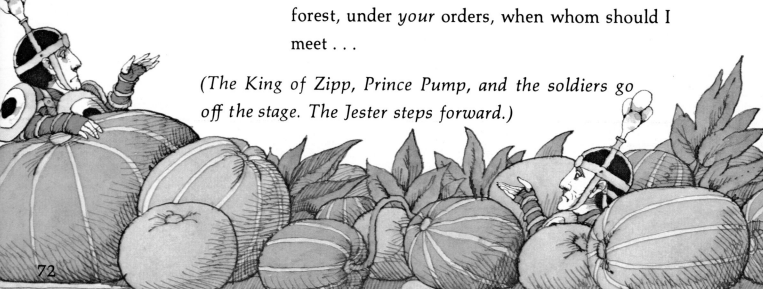

Jester: And the King of May
Could not understand
Why obblebumps grew
All over his land.

(The Jester sits down. The two soldiers of May come forward.)

First Soldier: I can't get rid of these things. They're everywhere.

Second Soldier: Shh! Here comes the King.

| King of May: *entering* | We can't fight a war when our cannons are covered with vines and these orange . . . ah . . . ah . . . whatzamajiggles. |
| King of May: | Obblebumps? |

King of May:
entering
We can't fight a war when our cannons are covered with vines and these orange . . . ah . . . ah . . . whatzamajiggles.

Princess Kin:
entering
Those whatzamajiggles are obblebumps.

King of May:
Obblebumps?

Princess Kin:
handing him a piece of pie
Yes, for obblebump pie. Try a piece.

King of May:
Obblebump pie? Yum. It's not half bad. Yum, not bad at all. In fact, it's delicious. So delicious, it's enough to make you forget about fighting and just think about eating instead!

Princess Kin:
Exactly! And I bet if you send a messenger to the King of Zipp, he'll feel very much the same way. Just think, Father. You and King Zipp will become famous for discovering obblebumps. All the other kings and queens in all the other kingdoms and queendoms will soon want obblebumps from you and King Zipp.

King of May:
Perhaps you're right. You always were a smart girl.

Prince Pump and Princess Kin invite Elise to join the two towns in celebrating Obblebump Day. The Jester stands at the center of the stage.

Jester: So that's how the war ended
Between Zipp and May.
They all joined together
For Obblebump Day!

(The Jester sits down at the side of the stage.)

Prince Pump: Isn't it wonderful? Obblebump Day!

Princess Kin: It sounds grand, doesn't it?

Elise: I have an idea. Let's not call these things obblebumps anymore. Let's name them after you.

Prince Pump: After me?

Princess Kin: After me?

Elise: Why, after both of you, of course. After you, Pump,

and after you, Kin. From now on, there will be no more obblebumps. We'll call them pumpkins instead!

Prince Pump: You don't say.

Elise: Yes, I do say.

Princess Kin: Oh no! Not again!

observation

noticing, study

All creatures learn by observation. With all their senses—touch, taste, sight, hearing, and smell—they pay careful attention to what's going on around them. For most animals, observation is a matter of life or death.

Keeping Watch in the Wild

Out of the woods comes a woodchuck and her four babies, about the size of kittens. There in the sunlight of the meadow, the youngsters roll and play, nipping and nuzzling one another.

Suddenly, as if by a silent signal, they rush to their mother. She is sitting

up with her head high, sniffing for danger.

In a short time, she comes down on

all fours and takes a mouthful of grass. The little ones reach up and take grass from her mouth. About every eight seconds, the mother raises her head to listen and to look for danger. The young woodchucks copy her.

The mother then begins another lesson. The den where they live is at the edge of the meadow. Suddenly, the mother woodchuck darts to the den. Her youngsters run after her. In seconds, they disappear into their underground home.

Soon the top of the mother's head appears, as she creeps slowly out of the den. At first only her eyes, her ears, and her nose can be seen. These are the woodchuck's three main ways of spotting danger, and they are all near the top of the woodchuck's head. So the woodchuck has to poke only a small part of its head out of its den to check for danger. If there is anything wrong, it can duck quickly inside.

In a few minutes the mother woodchuck goes back to the meadow, followed by her youngsters. They spend the rest of the day eating and running back to the den. But there is no danger. The mother isn't frightened by any strange sight or sound. She is simply teaching her young ones the habits of careful observation and the disappearing act that will make them masters of the meadow.

octopus

Two octopuses
walked down the street
arm
  in arm
    in arm
      in arm
        in arm
          in arm
            in arm
              in arm
                in arm
              in arm
            in arm
          in arm
        in arm
      in arm
    in arm
      in arm.

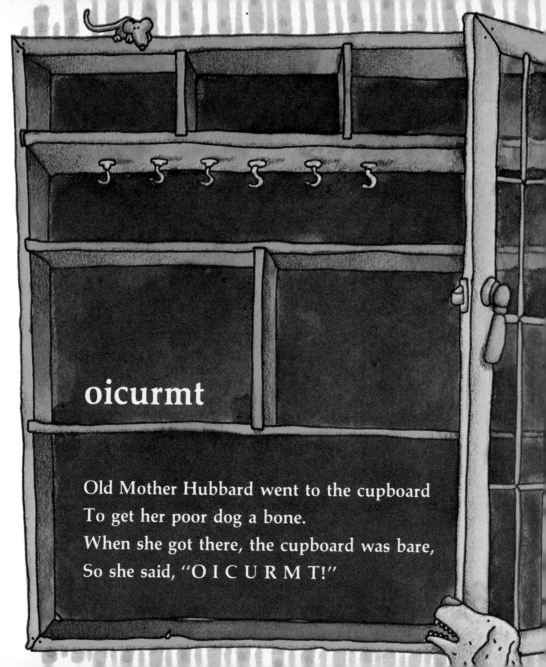

oicurmt

Old Mother Hubbard went to the cupboard
To get her poor dog a bone.
When she got there, the cupboard was bare,
So she said, "O I C U R M T!"

onyx

a stone that can be dyed, polished, and carved into figures and jewelry

The Case of the Black Onyx Cat

"What's a *curator*?" asked Janet.

"A curator is a person in charge of a museum," her grandmother answered. "Where do you see the word?" She put down the vase she was unpacking and walked over to Janet.

"It's here in the newspaper," Janet said. "A statue is missing from the museum. The curator says it's very old and valuable."

Janet's grandmother looked at the newspaper article. She was quiet a few moments. Then she said, "Ahhh." When her grandmother sighed like that, Janet knew that she was very interested in something.

"Yes, Janet. The statue is rare and very valuable. It is the famous Onyx Cat. The statue is thousands of years old. But it is most precious because of its legend," the old woman continued. "The Onyx Cat is thought to have strange powers. They say the cat cries a warning when someone is in danger."

"Really?" Janet asked excitedly. "Oh, I love mysteries. Tell me more!"

"The legend is that an emperor always kept the statue by his bed,"

Grandmother said. "When anyone came to harm him in the night, the Onyx Cat cried a warning. That is why the statue is so prized. But enough mystery for today, Janet. It is time for you to go to Mr. Lung's store. We need five-spice powder for dinner, tonight. And I need to get to work."

Grandmother reached for her brush and wrote down some characters on a piece of paper.

"Here, Janet. Give this shopping list to Mr. Lung."

As Janet left, Grandmother locked the door. Every afternoon she locked the art gallery doors, pulled down the window shades, and worked on the books in the office. But she always left the back door unlatched for Janet to come in to do her homework.

Q. W. Lung's store was one of

Janet's favorite places. There were hundreds of things to look at there—wind chimes, carved wooden toys, and paper dragons. But the back of the store held even more fascinating things.

One whole wall was covered with wooden drawers. There must have been one hundred of them, and each held a treasure. One drawer was filled with cloud ears. Another one was filled with star anise, and a third with dragon eyes. Janet knew, of course, that these were

names for different cooking spices. The cloud ears were really dried mushrooms. But they looked like what you would imagine a cloud's ear to be.

Janet handed Mr. Lung the list. One by one he opened drawers and weighed handfuls of spices on the scale. Last were the red pepper pods. Then he ground the spices into a fine, golden-red powder. He gave Janet a sniff. It tickled her nose.

In a few moments Janet was on her way with a small brown paper bag of five-spice powder in her pocket.

Janet slipped quietly through the back door into the office. She didn't want to disturb her grandmother. But then she noticed that Grandmother wasn't working at the desk. There was a strange voice coming from the art gallery.

"That's funny. Who's with Grandmother?" Janet wondered. She peeked into the gallery from behind the curtain.

There was Grandmother seated in the wicker chair beside the counter. A man in a gray coat and hat was standing over her. He was showing Grandmother something. But Janet couldn't see what it was.

"What about it, old woman?" the stranger asked in a threatening voice. "Are you going to cooperate or not? I'm sure one of your customers would pay good money for this. After all, it belonged to one of your emperors."

"And now it belongs to the museum," said Grandmother.

"The Onyx Cat!" thought Janet.

"I won't help you, no matter what you pay me," Grandmother said.

"All right, then," the stranger said.

"There are others around who will. You'll be sorry. It's your loss."

"It would be a greater loss to exchange my honesty for your money," said Grandmother. "You have my final word. I will not buy a stolen object. Not now or ever."

"Then remember to keep your mouth shut, or I will see that something happens to you," the man growled. "Understand?"

Grandmother nodded. The man wrapped something in newspaper and stuffed it into his pocket. He pulled down his hat and pulled up the collar of his coat.

Janet popped down behind a crate. The man walked out the office door without seeing her.

"Wow!" thought Janet. "He must be the one who stole the statue from the

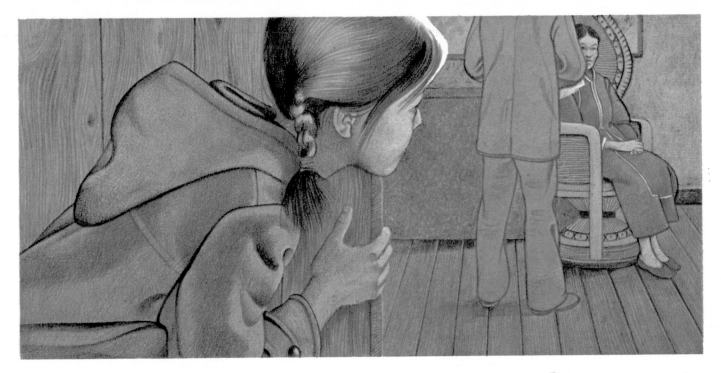

museum. If I follow him, maybe I can get it back. This is just what I've been waiting for—a real mystery!

Then Janet thought of how the strange man had threatened her grandmother.

"I'll fix that man," Janet said to herself. "How dare he try to harm Grandmother!" She sneaked out the office door. She was so excited, she didn't even think of the danger.

It was already getting dark. Janet followed the man in the gray coat down the narrow streets. Suddenly he turned a corner and disappeared. Janet looked around.

"Where'd he go?" she wondered.

Then Janet spotted a narrow alley. "He must be down there," she thought.

Janet peered into the alley. It seemed filled with mysterious shadows.

"Maybe there's a secret door or something," she said to herself. Janet tiptoed down the alley.

CLANG!

She tripped on a trash can cover. Janet ducked down and waited. All was still and quiet. She got up and walked on. But at the end of the alley, there was nothing but a brick wall.

"It's a dead end!" she said to herself. "But where could the man have gone?"

Suddenly from out of the shadows, the man appeared.

"Looking for me?" he asked in a deep voice.

Janet was shaking. Her back was to the wall. There was no way to escape.

"What am I going to do now?" she thought, crossing her fingers in her pocket. She could feel the bag of spices. How she wished she were safe at Mr. Lung's store!

Then suddenly out of the darkness came a piercing, screeching cry.

"Mrrrrouwl!"

A cat screamed. Janet couldn't see the cat, but its cry seemed to come from every side of the dark alley. The man stopped, startled.

"The Onyx Cat! It cried to save me!" Janet shouted.

At the same moment Janet stuck her hand in the paper bag and pulled out a fistful of spices. In a flash she threw it in the man's face.

"Yow!" he cried, as he put his

hands to his burning eyes. The tears blinded him. The more he rubbed, the more the spices stung.

But Janet didn't stay to look. She ran out of the alley and back to Grandmother's without stopping.

"Grandmother!" she called out. "It's true! It's true! The Cat! It saved my life!"

Janet stopped short. There were two police officers and a detective talking to her grandmother.

"What's this?" her grandmother asked. Janet explained. In a minute the police were on their way to the alley where Janet had followed the thief.

Later that night, Janet's grandmother got a call from the city police.

"That was the detective," Grandmother said to Janet as she hung up the phone. "The suspect has been caught. The statue was found in his coat pocket. Now the Onyx Cat is safely in the museum again. The detective wants us to come to the police station as soon as possible to identify the man."

"O.K." said Janet. "But then I'd like to go to the museum and thank the Onyx Cat for saving me."

"Thank a statue?" her grandmother asked, smiling. "It was probably just a frightened alley cat that helped you get away."

Janet smiled. "Oh Grandmother, don't be so sure."

orange

Many years ago on the other side of the world, some people discovered fruit trees growing wild. They called them "naranj trees," and they called the

fruit "naranj fruit." Word of this delicious discovery spread from person to person and from language to

apple tree is an apple. And what grows on a lemon tree is a lemon. So what grows on a naranj tree must be a naranj"—or, as people who spoke English heard it, an orange.

Soon oranges became known the world over. People began describing things that were the same color as the famous fruit as "orange."

language. Soon people began to call the fruit by the name of the tree. They probably thought, "What grows on an

ouch

outside

the opposite
of inside

I
am inside
looking outside
at the pelting
rain—
where
the outside world
is melting
upon my
window
pane.

Once uqon a time, there was a qrinter. The qrinter qrinted a little newsqaqer. But there was something pueer about the qaqer. Qeoqle couldn't read it! Everybody comqlained. The qrinter didn't know what to do.

"Why can't qeoqle read my qaqer?" he wondered. Finally he decided to go to the wise woman.

"I have a puestion," he told the wise woman. "In fact, I have a real qroblem. No one reads my newsqaqer. If this goes on, I'll be qoor! What can I do?"

"That's easy," said the wise woman. *"Mind your p's and q's."*

palindrome

What's a palindrome?

MOM and DAD and SIS are palindromes, but BROTHER and AUNT and GRANDPA are not.

EVE and NOON are palindromes, but MORNING and MIDNIGHT are not.

SNAP PANS and STRAW WARTS are palindromes. But TIN PANS and STRAWBERRIES are not.

What is a palindrome? AHA! Check your guess on page 334.

pancakes

hot cakes, griddle cakes flippers, and flapjacks

It is reported that Bill Wall tossed a pancake into the air 5,638 times. When people asked how he felt about winning the national pancake-tossing contest, Bill said, "Well, if I had lost, I would have felt waffle."

patent

If you are an inventor, you will want to get a patent. Then no one can copy your idea. A patent means that you are the only one who can make or sell your invention. Even though your invention is patented, it doesn't mean that anyone will buy it! Here are some crazy inventions that were patented. Do you think anyone bought them?

The Pedal-Speed

Prevent Sunburn!

Now you can stroll in the sunshine without worry. No more bright red face! No more peeling nose! Our patented sunshade hat is the invention you need.

Just strap on the wheels, and you're off! Enjoy a delightful spin around the park on your pedal-speed. Of course, it takes a bit of practice. But once you learn, you can skate all year round. The pedal-speed is light and easy to carry. Fresh-air fun for all ages!

The Portable Fish Server

Enjoy a delightful dinner party. An electric train runs from kitchen to table, so your dinner will always be piping hot.

The Improved Propeller Swimming Machine

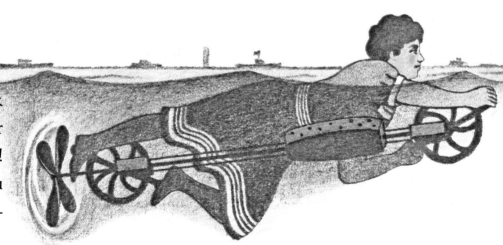

Simply marvelous! Crank the machine with your hands and feet. Whoosh! Through the water you go! A delight for the seaside vacationer.

The Practical Breeze-Machine

Do you have trouble getting things done in hot weather? It's easy with the practical breeze-machine. Just pump the foot pedal. The fan will keep you cool, and your hands will be free for reading or working.

The Pedal Shower Bath

Keep clean and keep trim, all at the same time! The patented pedal shower bath is a combination of bicycle and shower—the answer to all your needs. The harder you pedal, the more water pours over you.

PERFORMANCE

entertainment for an audience

In the movies, almost anything can happen! People can walk on walls, right up to the ceiling. And all sorts of monsters run, crawl, climb, and fly around the world.

While movies are certainly fun to watch, it can be even more interesting to see how they are made. If you take a look behind the scenes, you will learn some of the movie tricks.

Can this man really walk on walls and stand in midair? The picture certainly looks that way. But in fact, he is standing flat on the ground. It's the room that's sideways. All the furniture is nailed to the wall. And the man in the

chair is actually lying down on his back. Even his shoes are nailed to the floor. Turn the picture on its side, and you will see how the room really looks.

This giant sea monster is really a model. The diver it has captured is a model, too. But on the movie screen, both of them will look life-size. Many models used in the movies are tiny. But sometimes movie-makers build full-size mechanical monsters. Then real actors can be filmed with the monster.

Make-up is another kind of movie magic. It took more than three hours to put make-up on these actors. There was no time to take the make-up off for meals. So the actors had to wear it while they were eating, and then go back to work. They ate in front of mirrors to help them find their mouths. Drinking was easier — they could use straws.

This picture shows how a monster looks in the movies, . . .

...and this one shows how it looks in real life!

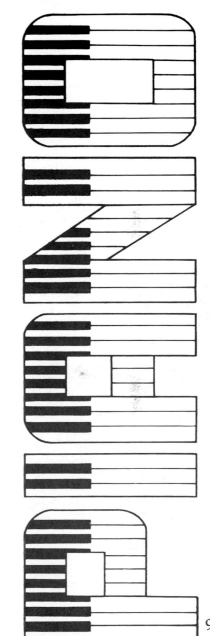

pick

Has the illustrator picked the right meaning for each sentence?

Sally asked Bill to pick a number from one to ten.

John picked up two friends on his way to work.

BIG **FIGHT** TONIGHT!

BIGGER **FIGHT** TONIGHT!

Susan picked a fight with Raymond.

Joan picked out a tune on the piano.

Before dinner, the lion carefully picked his teeth.

ping-pong

a game that sounds like this:

Chitchat — wigwag

rickrack — zigzag

knickknack — gewgaw

riffraff — seesaw

crisscross — flip-flop

ding-dong — tiptop

singsong — mishmash

King Kong — bong.

101

prehistoric

Think of all the people who have lived on this planet before you. What do you suppose their lives were like?

For five thousand years, people have left written records of their lives. They have written stories, plays, and poems about themselves and one another. They have made lists, sent letters, and kept journals. For five thousand years, people have been writing—on paper, clay, parchment, and stone. They have written with pens, sticks, quills, chisels, and brushes. All of these writings are part of history—the written record of human beings.

But what about all the thousands of years before writing was invented? The first human beings probably lived more than two million years ago—long before writing. This long, long period of time is called *prehistory*.

There are no written records from prehistoric times. But we can still learn what life was like. People made many important discoveries and inventions during prehistory.

One of the first human discoveries was how to make tools. Very early tools were made of stone. There were stone tools for chopping wood, cutting meat, and grinding seeds and nuts. There were stone spear points and arrowheads. Other tools were made from bone or wood. People made needles from bone to sew their clothing and tents. They made bone fishing hooks. They made wooden tent poles, axe handles, and fishing poles.

Another important prehistoric discovery was fire. Sometimes fires started naturally, when lightning struck a tree. But it was many, many years before humans learned to make fire. The earliest way to make fire was by striking certain kinds of stones together. Now humans could build a fire any time. Fire protected them from wild animals at night. Fire kept them warm in cold weather. And of course, fire was used for cooking.

How do we know about prehistoric people? We have found the stone tools that they used. We have found their fireplaces and bits of burnt wood from their fires. We have found the places where prehistoric people put up tents or built houses. We have found the caves where they sometimes lived. And deep inside the caves, we have found their paintings. We have even found the bones of some of these early people.

Tools and bones can show us how prehistoric people lived. But tools and bones can't tell us what early humans thought about or felt. We know they spoke languages, but no one knows what those languages were like. Because prehistoric people had no writing, all their words are lost forever.

promise

what you keep after giving it

The Promise of Spring

"Here. Throw these eggshells in with the corn. They make the chickens lay better eggs," Jose said, handing a pan full of eggshells to Rosa.

"Thanks, Grandpa," she said, dumping the shells into the pail of corn.

Jose opened the gate to the chicken coop and watched Rosa scatter the feed to the chickens. The rooster strutted by, and the hens squawked and pecked around Rosa's feet. Jane Austen, the barn cat, stretched lazily in the spring sunlight.

"Rosa is grown-up now," Jose thought as he watched his granddaughter. "But I remember buying her first pair of patent-leather shoes, just fifteen years ago. Yes, it's been fifteen years since we bought the farm."

Jose remembered the day it all began. The train he took to work had broken down because of a blizzard.

"You'll just have to stay home today," his wife, Juanita, said.

But, of course, Jose was much too stubborn to be kept home by a little snow.

"A little snow!" Juanita argued. "Jose, there's two feet of snow out there!"

But Jose's mind was set. He bundled up and began to walk the seven miles to work. It was hard to trudge through the snow, but Jose didn't feel tired. Instead, he felt wonderful. The cold, fresh air and sparkling sun filled him with energy. Before he knew it, he was laughing to himself.

He walked past snowdrifts with cars underneath. The blizzard had brought the city to a standstill. Its highways, bridges, and machines were wrapped in stillness.

"A great city may be mighty," he thought, "but tiny snowflakes are mightier."

The city had been good to him. He had come there poor, with two little children to feed. Today he had his own barbershop, a cozy apartment, and three grandchildren. But somehow, in that moment, the city no longer seemed the right place for him.

"I have lived here and grown here," he thought. "But now it is time for a different kind of growing. When winter turns to spring, I will leave the city for a new life."

107

Jose remembered a springtime of bird songs and blossoms, long ago in his boyhood. Inside, he was still that same boy. He loved watching the new leaves, the first flowers.

"I will move to the country," Jose decided.

Jose made himself a promise. He would sell the barbershop and buy a little farm. If anyone should tell him he was foolish, he would say, "I am seventy and old enough to think for myself."

All that day at the barbershop, Jose told his customers about his plan. Most of them just shook their heads.

It was very dark and cold by the time Jose walked up the steps to his apartment.

"Now, Jose, come in and get warm," said Juanita, opening the door.

"You should never have gone out this morning. You must be freezing. There's soup on the stove. Take a nice hot bath, and then we'll eat."

Jose just smiled as he got ready to eat. After dinner, he told her, "I have a surprise for you, Johnnie."

Juanita knew something must be up if Jose was using his favorite nickname for her.

"Surprise! It wouldn't surprise me if you caught a cold," she answered, a little gruffly.

But Jose knew that she was just trying to cover up her excitement and curiosity. So he said nothing for a minute.

Finally Juanita asked, "Well, come on now. What is it you're surprising me with, old man?"

Jose took her hand and said, "How

would you like living on a farm again, the way you did when you were a girl?"

"Those days are past," Juanita said. "If we had a million dollars and were twenty years younger, maybe I'd say yes. But quit your fooling, now. What's this all about?"

"It's about selling the shop and moving to the country," he answered.

"Jose!" Juanita exclaimed. "All those snowflakes have gotten into your head! You've become a crazy man. Don't you know you're seventy years old? And I'm no youngster, either!"

"Hush now, woman," Jose said. "It's just because we're getting old that we're going to move away from the city. We'll change our lives while we still have health and strength."

Jose spoke of the farm he wanted and of the fresh berries Juanita could pick. He spoke of horses and rabbits and a duck pond surrounded by green grass. He spoke of willow trees whispering in spring winds.

As he spoke, he could see a change in Juanita's eyes. Slowly, she entered into his dream of a new life. When he finished, Juanita laughed.

"Ah, you've always been a sweet talker," she said.

Before the evening was over, Juanita called everyone in the family and invited them for dinner the next day.

"We have a surprise for you," she told them excitedly.

The sky was just growing dark the next afternoon when Carlos, their son, arrived. Madelena, his wife, and little Rosa were with him.

"What's the surprise? My favorite

coconut-cream pie?'' Carlos asked as he kissed Juanita hello.

"No, a real surprise," Juanita said. "Come in and sit down. Jose wants to tell you about it himself."

Rosa, Jose's granddaughter, sat on his lap. Juanita sat by his side while Jose explained his plan.

"Buy a farm!" Carlos exclaimed. "Pop, I'm sorry to say this, but you can't do it."

"That's right," said Madelena. "We love you too much for you to go far away. We'd worry about you. Mom, you don't really mean it, do you?"

Juanita hesitated. "Maybe they're right, Jose. Last night you had me all caught up in your dream. But today is today. Let's just remember the dream and leave it that way."

Jose just looked at Juanita. He put his granddaughter down. He said nothing and walked out of the room. As he left, he could hear Juanita whisper to the others, "Don't worry. He'll get over it."

Jose went down into the basement to his workbench. He took some paper and began drawing. He was so busy with his work that he didn't hear the door creak. He didn't hear the little girl with new patent-leather shoes step up behind him.

"What's that, Grandpa?" Rosa asked, peeking over his shoulder.

"It's a drawing," answered Jose, "a plan for building a hen house."

"What kind of hens are you going to have on your farm, Grandpa?" asked Rosa.

Jose turned around. "So you want to visit me at the farm, huh?" His big, wrinkled hand closed tightly around Rosa's small one. All at once Jose felt joy inside again as he shared his dream with his granddaughter.

"Can we have red hens? They're my favorites," Rosa said.

"I promise," Jose replied. "I promise you, and I promise me, too."

It had been a long time since then. Jose closed the chicken coop gate. He put his arm around Rosa, and they walked back to the farmhouse. It was a beautiful day. Spring was about to burst into summer.

"You know, Grandpa," Rosa said, "I always did like the red hens the best."

punctuation

marks that tell you to ask? exclaim!
pause, short'n "speak" or stop.

Period

When you come to the end of a written thought
You just sign-off with a polka dot.

Question Mark

Symbol of all I wish I knew
Polka dot under a curlicue. . . .

Comma

A sentence is a band of words
Going for a walk.
A comma is a pause for breath
Taken as you talk.
And when you write, a comma is
Set down just because
It is time you gave your reader a
Little chance to pause.

Apostrophe

Apostrophes are floating commas that show who owns a thing,
As in <u>mamma's</u> shoe, <u>boy's</u> hat, <u>man's</u> glove, <u>girl's</u> ring.
Apostrophes can shrink words as do not into <u>don't</u>,
Have not into <u>haven't</u> and will not into <u>won't</u>.

Quotation Marks

Let you know who
Remarked, harked, or barked.
"Bow wow," said Fred.
"Hark!" shouted Ferdinand.
"What's that?" asked Mabel.
"I know," said Pomfret.
"Tell us!" said Georgia.
"Company!" exclaimed Tootsie.
"Oh dear," cried Wally.
"Who?" asked Bonny.
"Who knows?" answered Paulette.

Exclamation

At the end of a word or a line to excite,
Scare or command it's proper to write   !

115

The Pirate Flag

Take turns reading the following story out loud with a buddy. One of you should read the words. The other should read the punctuation marks. How? Just follow this simple code.

. **Bong**   , **Hummm**

" **Beep**   ! **Boing**

? **Ding**   ' **Poof**

The Pirate Flag

"What ho!" cried Pirate Pat, sitting in the crow's nest. "Thunder and lightning! There's a treasure ship. Look lively, my cutthroats!"

Pirate Pat slid down to the ship's deck.

"How far away is the ship?" asked Blackbeard, the pirate captain.

"We'll meet the ship before the sun sets," said Pirate Pat. "What are your orders, Captain?"

"Mates! Listen!" called Blackbeard. "Put up a false flag. Stay well hidden. When we're almost upon them, we'll raise our flag. Raise the pirate flag! That'll be a beautiful surprise, hey?" And Blackbeard laughed a deep, mean, nasty, chilling, scary, gruesome, eerie, wild, awful, terrifying, pirate laugh.

Q's are weird O's.

117

quack

a person who pretends to be a doctor but isn't

Once there was a clever but lazy man who wished to be rich.

"Now, where can I get some money?" he thought to himself. "The king has more money than anyone else. Let's see if I can get him to give me a little!"

So he set off to see the king. He passed through many villages, and everywhere he saw people who had aches or pains or colds or fevers.

"Hmmm," he thought. "That gives me an idea. What this country needs is a doctor. Now, of course, I don't know anything about medicine. But then, neither does the king!"

When the lazy man reached the palace, he went before the king and said, "Your Majesty, how can you be a great king when you do not take care of your people? There are so many sick people in your kingdom! Fortunately, I am a famous doctor. I can cure all the sick people, and then everyone will praise you for being such a great king."

The king was worried. "I had no idea there were so many sick people in my kingdom," he said. "If you can cure them all, I will make you rich beyond your wildest dreams. But if you do not cure them, I will have your head cut off."

"Your Majesty, I accept your conditions," said the quack.

Then the king called the royal herald and said, "Herald, go and invite all the sick people in the kingdom to come and be cured by the great doctor."

The herald set out at once. He traveled all over the kingdom blowing his trumpet and shouting, "Hear ye! Hear ye! The king invites all the sick

119

people in the kingdom to come to the palace to see the greatest doctor in the world!"

And all the sick people in the kingdom came to the palace as fast as they could.

The quack said to one of the king's servants, "Light a fire in the biggest room of the palace."

The servant went off and lit a roaring fire in the fireplace of the biggest room in the palace, as he had been told.

When the room was ready, the quack said, "Now bring all the sick people here. Then close the door and leave me alone with them."

When the quack was alone with the sick people, he said, "My friends, I am the greatest doctor in the whole wide world. There is no sickness that I cannot cure. I promise to cure you all, if you take the medicine that I give you. What do you say?"

"Give us the medicine, doctor! We'll take it!" everyone shouted.

"Good," said the quack. "First, I'm going to take the sickest person in the room and throw that person into the fire. Then with the ashes, I'll make the medicine to cure you all."

The quack looked around the room. Finally he said to one man, "You, my friend, look like the sickest person in the room."

"Who, me?" asked the man. "Not at all. I'm not sick. In fact, I feel great."

"You feel great? You're not sick? Well, what are you doing here with all the sick people? Get out!" the quack ordered.

The poor fellow left the room at once. The king was waiting outside.

"Are you all better, my friend?" asked the king. "Are you cured?"

"Oh, yes, your Majesty, completely cured," said the man. And he left the palace as fast as he could.

The quack looked around the room again. "Good woman, you look for all the world like the sickest person in the room."

"Who, me? Oh, no, doctor!" the woman exclaimed. "I've never felt better in my life. I don't feel the least bit sick."

"If you don't feel the least bit sick, what are you doing here?" demanded the quack. "Go on—out with you!"

So the sick woman left the room at once. As she hurried toward the palace door, the king stopped her and asked, "Well, now—how do you feel? Are you all better?"

"Oh, yes, your Majesty," said the woman. "I feel much better, thank you." And she left the palace as fast as she could.

A third sick person left the room, then a fourth, then a fifth. They all told the king that they were completely cured and had never felt better.

Soon all the other sick people had left the room, each one saying, "I'm well!" "I feel much better!" "I'm cured!" "I don't feel sick any more!" And each one left the palace and went home on the run, without looking back.

Finally, the quack left the room and said to the king, "Your Majesty, I have succeeded. There are no longer any sick people in your kingdom."

quadruped

a four-legged animal

The Quagga Is Dead

"The quagga is dead," the old zebra said.
"We have all seen the last of that poor quadruped.
He was striped like a zebra from middle to head.
But from middle to tail, he was all white instead,
Like a snowy white donkey. Poor Quagga is dead.

"Oh, weep for the quagga!" the old zebra said.
"He was gentle and shy and very well-bred.
He was light on his feet and gay-spirited.
But now he is gone. His days have all fled.
And if that was *his* fate, then what lies ahead
For me and my friends, now that Quagga is dead?"

quarter

Gather your buddies to watch this trick.

Put a dime on a small square of paper and trace it with a pencil. Cut

out the circle to make a dime-sized hole.

Tell your buddies you can push a quarter through the dime-sized hole without tearing the paper.

Here's how you do it. Fold the paper across the

hole with the quarter inside.

It will now be simple to push the coin through the hole.

Try this trick with a half-dollar through a nickel-sized hole.

query

a question

Father,
Where do giants go to cry?

To the hills
Behind the thunder?
Or to the waterfall?
I wonder.

(Giants cry.
I know they do.
Do they wait
Till nighttime too?)

quest

a long search for something

Loch Ness is the deepest lake in Scotland. The waters of Loch Ness are deep, dark, and cold. And for more than a thousand years, people have talked about a strange, unknown beast that lives in these waters.

There have always been stories of a dragon or a monster in Loch Ness. Hundreds of people claim to have seen a large, dark, snake-like animal swimming in the loch. Some people think the creature might be a kind of dinosaur. But many others do not believe it exists at all.

Scientists have begun a quest for the Loch Ness monster. Does it exist? What kind of animal is it? Is there more than one monster in the loch?

One of the best ways to prove that a monster exists is to take a picture of it. This photograph is the first picture of the beast that was ever taken.

But the photo is blurry. Does it really show the head and neck of the monster? Or is it just a log or a bird?

The quest for the Loch Ness monster is difficult. The monster seems to stay under the water most of the time, where it is very dark and murky. Even with bright lights, a diver can see only a few feet ahead. So in recent years, the scientists have begun to hunt for the monster in new ways. They decided to test the deep lake with sonar.

Sonar is used in submarines to tell if there is anything ahead that can't be seen in the dark water.

The sonar equipment sends out a sound. When the sound hits something, the sound will bounce back like an echo. From these echoes, scientists can tell what size the *something* is and how fast it is moving. Sonar has been used in Loch Ness for several years. It seems to show that a number of large, fast-moving *somethings* live in the loch. But sonar does not show what they look like.

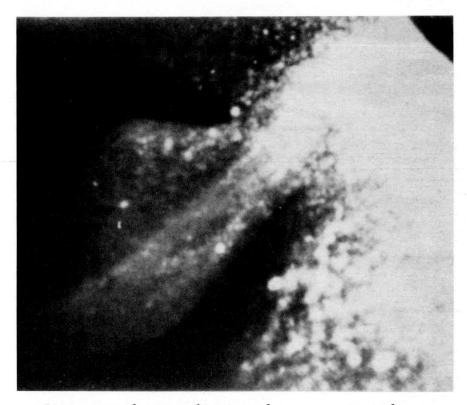

Scientists have also tried to use underwater cameras in Loch Ness. But because the water is so murky, the pictures show only things that are very close. Cameras have been left underwater, set to go off if anything large moves nearby. One of these underwater pictures seems to show part of an animal with a diamond-shaped flipper.

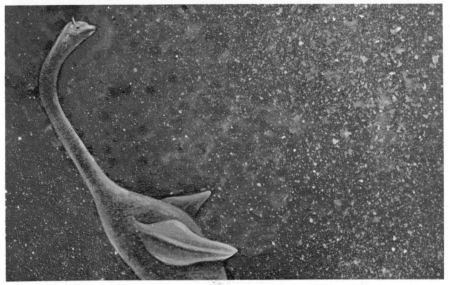

Some other under-water pictures also show unexplained objects. Are these really pictures of the monster?

Many scientists see in this photograph a long, curving neck and the front part of a large body with two flippers. The neck curves back into the shadows, and it can't be seen very clearly. Below the photograph is a drawing that shows what the animal may look like. But other people say that there is nothing in the photo except a cloud of bubbles or an old sunken ship.

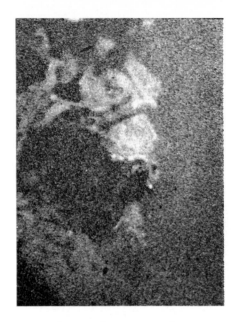

This photograph may show the monster's head. Its mouth is open, and the head has two small, horn-like bumps on top. An illustrator has drawn a picture of the head. Not everyone agrees that this is a picture of the monster. Some people think it is only a photograph of a carved wooden dragon. Carvings of dragons, like the one in the last picture, were often used to decorate ships long ago. But other scientists argue that the sonar showed living, moving objects. In fact, something very big was moving close enough to the underwater camera to flip the camera upside-down.

Could there still be a dinosaur alive in Loch Ness? Or is it some other large animal that scientists have never studied? The quest may go on for many years.

quiet

Quiet

it says

in the library

Quiet

and what I want to know is

what's quiet

inside the books

with all those

ideas and words

Myra Cohn Livingston

shouting?

QUILT

A quilt is a special kind of blanket. It has a top piece, a bottom piece, and some stuffing in between. The stuffing can be cotton, wool, or feathers. The top and bottom pieces are stitched together to make a lot of separate little pockets for the stuffing, so it won't all lump up.

The earliest quilts were just sewn-up sacks stuffed with leaves, grass, or straw. They were used for mattresses or cushions, as well as blankets.

Later, people began to decorate their quilts. When they were making a new quilt, they stitched some colored scraps of cloth together to make the top piece. If they already had a plain quilt, they sewed some colored patches on the top. Sometimes the colored patches were stitched together every which way to make a "crazy quilt." On other quilts, the pieces made a picture.

Quilt-making was something that people often did together, because it takes a lot of sewing to make a quilt. Family members would work together on a quilt, or several families would meet to sew and keep each other company. These larger gatherings were called "quilting bees."

A quilt is bright pieces of love and peace sewn together for warmth and comfort, for drinking cocoa under, for reading a book under, and for sharing a secret with brothers and sisters under.

Across Grandmother's knees
A kindly sun
Laid a yellow quilt.

QZ13

A code name for a super-secret agent

Secret Agent QZ13 had just finished another assignment. Now it was time for a fishing vacation. But the minute QZ13 baited her hook, her Secret Agent's multipurpose fishing pole began to talk. A tiny two-way radio was hidden inside the handle.

Headquarters was calling her. Using spy code language like "GRIX BIBBLE KERPLOP," Chief Benson told her that the smallest but most dangerous super-weapon ever invented—the Crumble Bomb—had been stolen. Simon La Greedy was holding the bomb at his hideout in Alaska. He was demanding one hundred million dollars as ransom.

"And," the Chief added, "Simon says that if he sees any kind of gang coming toward his hideout, he'll explode the super-weapon. He'd rather die than

let himself be captured. The bomb is no
bigger than a chicken egg. But it is
powerful enough to cause the whole
world to crumble like a cookie.''

"Don't worry, Chief. I'm on my
way," QZ13 replied.

A few minutes later, she pressed a
red button in her sports car. Presto!
Wings slid out from under the doors,
changing her car into a jet plane.

QZ13 headed for Alaska. But when
she reached La Greedy's hideout, there
was no place to land. QZ13 set the
controls on automatic to send the plane
back to headquarters. Then she para-
chuted down.

When she landed, she found herself nose to nose to nose with Simon La Greedy and his servant, Boris.

Simon was holding what looked like a muddy-blue egg.

"Don't move," he growled, "or I'll crumble the world."

QZ13 stood still. "If you do," she reminded Simon, "you'll also destroy yourself."

"Ho, ho, ho!" laughed Simon. "Do you think we care about that? We'd be happy to see the world end if we can't have things our own way. Boris, let's make our unwelcome visitor uncomfortable."

Boris pulled a lever and a trapdoor opened. QZ13 fell through.

Thinking fast, she knocked her Secret Agent's multipurpose E-Z tread shoes against each other in midair. Click! Click! Before she landed, a dozen hidden springs popped out from the bottom of each shoe.

Ping! Ping! QZ13 bounced safely across the floor like a kangaroo. For the moment, she was safe. But she was still a prisoner in an underground cage.

QZ13 took off her Secret Agent's multipurpose waterproof wrist watch and pulled the winding stem.

Out came a thin mini-saw. Quickly, she sawed her way out of the cage. Outside was a dark, narrow tunnel.

QZ13 pulled out the small but powerful flashlight built into her Secret Agent's multipurpose friendship ring. The tunnel led to a locked steel door. She picked the lock with an ordinary hairpin. She slipped through the door and found herself in the kitchen. There was a sudden noise. It was Boris fixing lunch. QZ13 flattened herself against a wall. She pulled her Secret Agent's multipurpose ballpoint pen from her pocket. Aiming it at Boris, she clicked the top. Whish!

A thin jet of smoky green gas squirted across the room. Immediately Boris sank to the floor, fast asleep. When the green cloud vanished, QZ13 locked him inside the tunnel.

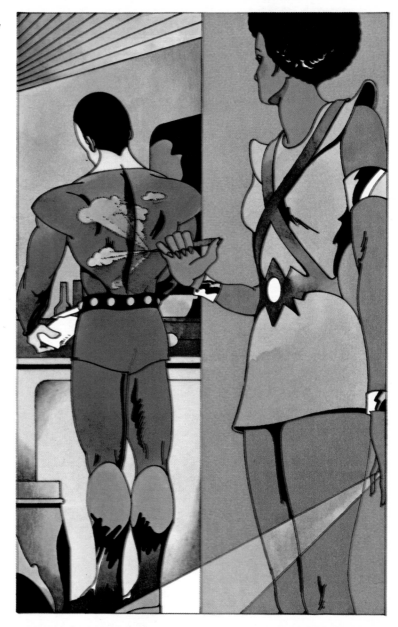

She took one egg from the refrigerator.

Using her Secret Agent's multi-purpose scarf pin, she punched a tiny hole in the plastic ink tube of her pen. The ink dripped onto the egg.

Meanwhile Simon La Greedy was having his lunch. The Crumble-Bomb lay on a thick pink cushion in front of his plate.

Somehow QZ13 had to get her hands on it before Simon could.

Holding the ink-stained egg above her head, QZ13 stepped into the room and shouted, "Here!" She tossed the muddy-blue egg toward Simon. "You'd better catch this thing before it hits."

Simon didn't have time to think. He screamed and toppled over backwards. The egg splattered on his shiny bald head.

QZ13 moved quickly. She carefully slipped the real Crumble-Bomb into her pocket. Then she ripped off Simon's socks and tied the crook's hands behind his back. Using her Secret Agent's multipurpose, transistor-radio belt buckle, she called headquarters.

"BLIP KAZOOM HUT FROBBLE," she said. Which meant, "I have the Crumble-Bomb and the two meatballs who stole it. Send a helicopter to the hideout."

Later, as soldiers were taking Simon and Boris away, Chief Benson landed in his private helicopter.

Before he could say a word, the super-spy QZ13 gently handed over the Crumble-Bomb.

"Good work," Chief Benson said. "You've done it again, QZ13. I knew you would. You always finish whatever you start."

QZ13 smiled and jumped into the chief's private whirlybird.

Chief Benson shouted, "What do you think you're doing?"

QZ13 waved good-by. "GRUMBLE DIP ZIDDLE," she yelled above the roar of the helicopter. Which meant, "That's right, Chief. I always finish whatever I start. So I'm going back to finish my vacation and catch some fish!"

141

Well, then,

let's begin!

radio

where you hear music, news, and weather

No Nonsense

Jack and Miss Carswell were sitting across from each other in the living room while he listened to the story she had chosen to read to him that night. She always read him a story before bedtime, and usually the stories were boring enough to make him sleepy. But even a boring story was better than going to bed early; so he listened.

Jack remembered Susie Finch, his

last sitter. She had read better stories, he decided. Susie, unlike Miss Carswell, had had a lively imagination. Therefore, she had been frightened by every strange sound.

"What's that noise?" she would say, stopping right in the middle of the bedtime story. "That sounds like some-body trying to get in!"

"It does not. It's only the wind," Jack would say. "Go on with the story."

Jack was eight years old now, and he didn't really think that he needed a babysitter. But his parents disagreed—although they were careful not to say "babysitter" anymore. They just said "sitter." Jack had enjoyed being the brave one while Susie was the scaredy-cat, but finally his parents had decided that Susie was too imaginative to be a

good sitter. How could she take care of Jack if she was scared of everything? Miss Carswell had taken Susie's place.

Miss Carswell was not young. She needed glasses to read, and she wore clunky shoes. She always carried a large, ugly purse. Jack's parents thought she was an excellent sitter, especially after Susie Finch. Miss Carswell took her sitting very seriously. There was no nonsense about her.

Miss Carswell was the first sitter Jack had ever had who was not young. Jack wondered why anyone so old would want to be a sitter, and since he was very curious, he asked her.

She smoothed her plain brown skirt and answered his question right away. "I can spend my evenings just as pleasantly here as I would at home, reading books and listening to music. And I welcome the chance to make some pin money."

"What do you need pins for?" asked Jack.

"That's just an expression," said Miss Carswell.

Jack almost liked her. At least he thought she was funny. Sometimes after he had gone to bed, he would get to thinking about her and the way she did things, and he would laugh out loud.

"Is something the matter?" she would call down the hallway.

"No," Jack would answer.

"Then go to sleep," she would say. And he would.

Miss Carswell was certainly different from Susie Finch. The things that had scared Susie didn't bother Miss Carswell at all. Just to see if he could throw a scare into her, Jack sometimes acted nervous on purpose. But it usually didn't work. So he was glad one night when he heard a distant swooshing sound that was really quite odd. It was not like anything he could remember hearing before. Maybe this time he could scare Miss Carswell.

"Hey, what's that strange noise?" he said, turning his head to show that he was listening to something.

"What is what?" she asked, looking up from the book. She listened carefully.

"It sounds as if a giant is coming," said Jack, because it really did if you used your imagination a little. But Miss Carswell never used her imagination, because there was no nonsense about her. She frowned at him firmly.

"It's only the wind," she said and went back to her reading.

But the noise became louder, like a distant roaring and grinding, and not so distant at that.

"Listen! It sounds like a giant taking giant steps," insisted Jack. (Because he was named Jack, he had always thought he would enjoy scrambling down a beanstalk with a giant huffing after him.)

Miss Carswell closed the book.

"Nonsense," she said. "It's just the wind. However, it does sound like a very strong wind. I'll tell you what we'll do. Let's go down to the basement and turn on that big radio your father has down there. Perhaps we can get a weather report."

Miss Carswell rose, picked up her purse, took Jack by the hand, and

walked out to the kitchen and across to the basement door. She opened the door, closed it behind them, led Jack down the steps, told him to sit down, and turned on the radio.

Even though they were in the basement now, they could still hear the noise, and it was getting louder and louder. Miss Carswell fiddled with the radio and found a station. It did not come in clearly. But between the crackles and hisses in the radio, they heard a few words.

"The tornado *zzzap* is only *scratch zizzle* miles away *pop*," said the radio announcer. "Tornado warnings *crackle* have been sent *zzapp*."

"What's a tornado?" Jack asked Miss Carswell. He hoped it was a kind of giant.

"Well," she said, "a tornado—"

Before she could say any more, the roaring became very, very loud. The radio went dead, and the lights went off.

"The giant is here! The giant is here!" shouted Jack, jumping up and down with excitement.

"Nonsense," said Miss Carswell in the darkness. "Don't be alarmed. I have a flashlight in my purse. I always carry one for just these emergencies."

She got out the flashlight and shined it toward Jack. But already the roaring and grinding was getting softer. It was moving away.

"The giant's leaving!" cried Jack. "He's leaving! I want to see him!" He

hoped that for once there really was a giant stomping around.

"Don't be silly, Jack," said Miss Carswell. The noise was already far, far away. She took him by the hand, pointing her light carefully ahead of them up the steps to the door. She opened the door, and they stepped into the kitchen.

Every one of the kitchen windows was broken. The back door was smashed, too. They walked over to the hole where the door had been and looked out. Where was the porch? Every stick and brick of it was gone! And the apple tree lay on its side with its roots in the air. Jack looked up at Miss Carswell, and Miss Carswell looked down at him.

"You see?" she said. "I told you it was only the wind." Miss Carswell was never one for nonsense.

rain

Spring rain:
Everything just grows
More beautiful.

A summer shower;
The exhausted horse
Comes to life again.

This long afternoon!
The sound of the rain
Says what I think.

Stars on the pond;
Again the splattering
of late winter rain.

rectangle

I am the robot McJangular.
My body's completely rectangular.
(You can see I'm no square,
Like my friend over there.)
Don't you think that I look quite spectangular?

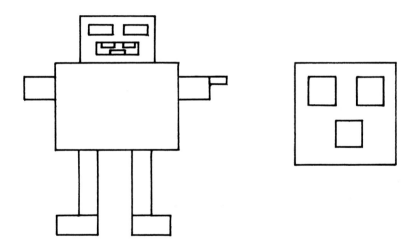

McJangular   His friend, the Square

How many rectangles would you need to
make another robot just like McJangular?
If you can't figure it out, look on page 334.

relish

Relish has two meanings:
1. To enjoy something
2. A mixture of chopped pickles

Bill Wall was asked how he
liked his new job in the pickle
factory. Bill replied, "I don't
relish it!"

return

to put back, replace, or give back

Finders Keepers

"Hey, Ralph! That's mine!" yelled Orlando, racing down the school steps.

Ralph clutched Orlando's baseball and said, "Tough break. I found it under the bushes. Finders keepers. Come on, guys. Let's play ball."

"But I left it out here at noon. There wasn't time to look for it then," objected Orlando. "The bell rang, and you know what Ms. Jackson says if we're late."

"Finders keepers," Ralph said again as he turned away.

Orlando kicked a clump of dirt. "So it's finders keepers," he thought as he trudged home. He slapped his mitt and remembered again the sting of the ball on the day he had caught it. It had been a home run at his first major league game. And it had come straight at him. He had raised his mitt. And plunk! His hand had stung, but the ball was his. And now Ralph had it.

"Is something wrong?" asked his mother as Orlando entered the house. For a moment Orlando considered telling her. But what good would it do?

"Nothing I can change," Orlando thought. And he hurried past.

The next morning he stopped to

watch Ralph and the others playing ball
again. "With my baseball," muttered
Orlando.

Ralph stepped up to bat. One
pitch—crack! Ralph's hard line drive
shot out to right field. Ralph rounded
first base and was heading for second as
the bell rang. In spite of his mood,

Orlando grinned. Everyone was coming at once. Ms. Jackson's lecture about being on time had worked. He turned to go inside, not looking at Ralph.

Moments later in their homeroom Orlando heard Ralph's hushed, angry voice.

"Hey, Barb. I thought you had my mitt," Ralph hissed. "My dad paid fifteen dollars for that mitt. If it's lost, I'll be in trouble."

"So Ralph's mitt was left outside," thought Orlando. "It would serve him right if somebody took it. Wasn't finders keepers Ralph's own motto?" Then Orlando heard Ralph's name called.

"Ralph, did you hear my question?" repeated Ms. Jackson.

"No," admitted Ralph in a quiet voice.

"We'll discuss this at noon. Wait a few minutes after the bell," said Ms. Jackson. "All right, Ralph?"

"Yes," Ralph whispered.

"It will be a long morning for Ralph," thought Orlando. He felt a little sorry for him.

When the noon bell rang, Orlando hurried outside. Some days he wished he stayed for lunch instead of going home; today was one of them. Now he wouldn't know what happened with Ralph until later.

As he passed behind home plate, he slowed. Beside a bush, nearly hidden, lay Ralph's mitt.

"It would serve Ralph right if I took it," muttered Orlando.

He started to leave, but paused. Why not? Ralph had something of his. He would have something of Ralph's.

He snatched the mitt from the grass and ran home.

As he entered the house, he shoved the mitt under his jacket and tossed both on a chair. There was no sense in getting his mother upset.

"You're quiet today," said his mother as he ate. "Did you have a hard morning?"

"No," he said quickly. To his relief she said nothing more.

On the way back to school, Orlando thought, "I should have left the mitt home. Then I wouldn't have to face Ralph with it." But why shouldn't he face Ralph? The mitt was his, just as much as the baseball was Ralph's.

"Hey, Orlando," called Ralph, walking toward him. "You went home for lunch. Did you see my mitt when you left?"

155

Orlando took a deep breath and pulled out the mitt. Ralph would find out sometime anyway. "I found a mitt, but it's mine now. Finders keepers. Remember?"

Ralph's face turned pale, and his fists clenched and unclenched at his side. Orlando stood still and waited. Suddenly Ralph turned away and pushed through the group that had gathered. He disappeared into the school.

"Good going, Orlando," called Barb. "That fixed him."

"I never thought I'd see Ralph cry," said someone else.

Orlando tried to smile as everyone congratulated him. He had expected to feel good about getting back at Ralph. But he didn't. What was wrong with him?

Finally the others drifted away. Orlando silently stared at the yard. No one was playing ball. Ralph had the only baseball today. Sadly, Orlando walked into the school.

"I never thought I'd see Ralph cry." The words echoed in Orlando's mind. Even when accidentally hit with a bat, Ralph hadn't cried. For a mitt, he did cry. It served him right with his finders-keepers idea, Orlando told himself. It was a rotten idea, though. Look how it made both of them feel.

Their homeroom was empty when Orlando entered. It was five minutes until the bell. He knew what he must do while he had a chance. He went over to Ralph's desk and stuffed the mitt inside.

A minute later, Orlando rushed back outside to wait for the bell. It seemed like forever until it sounded.

157

Orlando walked quickly into the room and saw Ralph already seated. That would mean Ralph had found the mitt. Slipping into his own desk, Orlando waited for Ralph to speak. Nothing came.

"Well, I don't care," Orlando thought. "At least my conscience is clear. Ralph will have to live with his."

Opening his desk, Orlando reached for his math book—and gasped. There was his baseball! His eyes met Ralph's. Ralph grinned and bent over his book. Joy filled Orlando as he touched the baseball. Ralph had taken good care of it. When had Ralph returned it? Before or after he found his mitt? Well, it didn't really matter. More important, Orlando had a feeling neither he nor Ralph would play finders keepers again.

reword

to say the same thing in a different way

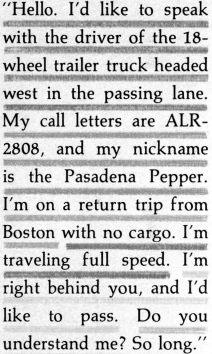

"Breaker westbound 18 in the show-off lane, this is ALR-2808, the one and only Pasadena Pepper. I'm on a bounce-around out of Bean Town, hauling post holes and pedaling with both feet. We're hanging onto your mudflaps and knocking on the back door. You got a copy on me? Westbound and just looking around."

"Hello. I'd like to speak with the driver of the 18-wheel trailer truck headed west in the passing lane. My call letters are ALR-2808, and my nickname is the Pasadena Pepper. I'm on a return trip from Boston with no cargo. I'm traveling full speed. I'm right behind you, and I'd like to pass. Do you understand me? So long."

river

plop plop
drops of rain
atop a mountain
trickle and spill
and fill a creek
that rumbles and bubbles
and tumbles into
a dashing splashing stream
which winds and finds its way
through meadows then
roars and pours into a waterfall
that smoothly glides and slides into a widening river
with spreading fingers reaching for the endless sea.

160

RODEO

a show where people compete for prizes in bronco riding, cattle roping, and other events

1. Where I come from, a rodeo is something to get excited about, like the Fourth of July, the traveling circus, or the World Series. In fact, a rodeo is like all of those rolled into one big, long, loud, colorful, breathtaking extravaganza. And last year the biggest rodeo of the summer took place near my town. I had decided that I wasn't going to be just an onlooker this time. This year I was going to enter one of the rodeo events myself.

2. When I told my parents what I had decided, they weren't too happy about it. Some of the events are really dangerous. But they knew that I could ride, and they knew how much I wanted to try it—just one time. So they finally agreed, but they made me promise to be careful. They said that they would come and cheer for me.

3. I wanted to get a special outfit for the rodeo. Even though there's no official uniform for people who compete in the rodeo, there are certain clothes that just about everybody wears. Most rodeo people wear a fancy cowboy hat, a bright, long-sleeved shirt, a tooled leather belt, cowboy boots with spurs, and—most important—some good riding gloves. The clothes are partly for show, but partly for safety, too. The heavy gloves and boots protect you.

4. When the day of the rodeo

finally arrived, I was all set and ready to go. We got to the arena early to register. The woman behind the registration desk gave me an entry form to fill out. It had all the events on it, like calf roping, bulldogging, and broncobusting. I had finally decided to sign up for the toughest, most exciting event of all—bull riding. I took a deep breath, handed in my form, and paid my entry fee. There. I'd done it.

5. The woman at the desk smiled and told me to sit in the grandstand and enjoy the show until I heard my name called over the loudspeaker. I went to the grandstand as she suggested. But it was hard to watch the show when all I could think about was riding that bull. What would it be like? Would I be able to stay on? What if I were thrown off? Why did I ever sign up to ride a bull?

Was I crazy? Hey, was that *my* name coming from the loudspeaker? It was. My legs seemed to move by themselves, carrying me over to the chutes and riders. This was it.

6. I saw the huge Brahma bull in the pen. I knew he was mine because I was to ride next. I tightened the straps around my gloves at the wrists. Two cowboys lifted me into the chute and onto the bull's back. Then they passed a rope twice around the bull and pulled it tight over my hand—that's how you hold on while you're riding a bull. As they were lifting me up, I glanced across the arena into the grandstands. In the blur of faces, I thought I saw my family.

7. "Just hang in there, buddy," someone said, "and don't let go." Then they opened the gate. The next thing I

knew, I was out there on a two-thousand-pound bull that was bucking and kicking and twisting. The whole world rocked and pounded and wobbled and bounced. Every time the bull bucked, all of my bones seemed to come loose and knock together. The eight-second time limit seemed like hours. All that time, I wasn't aware of a single sound. I'm sure that the crowd was cheering, since they cheer for everybody. But I didn't hear them. All that I could see clearly was the back of the charging bull's neck. I just held on and waited for the buzzer. When it sounded at last, I let go of the rope, and my ride was over.

8. Somehow I'd made it. Even if I never do it again, I know how it feels to be a real rodeo rider.

roller coaster

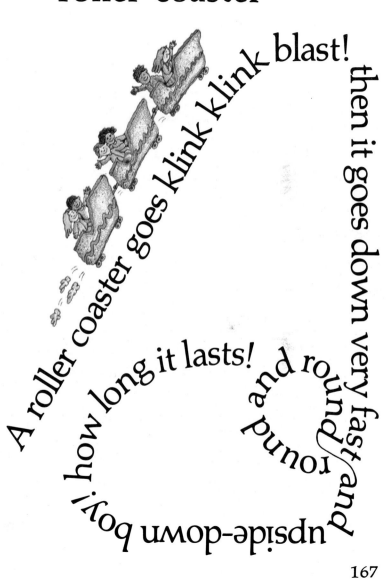

A roller coaster goes klink klink klink blast! then it goes down very fast and round and round and upside-down boy! how long it lasts!

167

S

I want a sandwich with some ham and some cheese and some

some tomato and some lettuce and some mayonnaise and

butter and some mustard and some salt and some pepper and

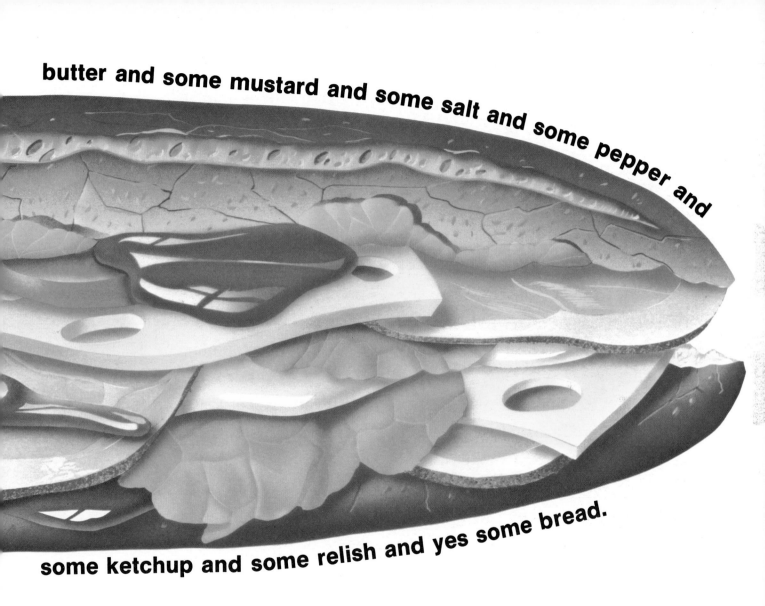

some ketchup and some relish and yes some bread.

The sandwich was invented about two hundred years ago in England by the earl of a town named Sandwich. The Earl of Sandwich liked to play cards. Sometimes he would not get up from a game to go sit down at dinner. What he wanted was a meal that he could eat with one hand while playing cards with the other.

"Why not put my supper between two slices of bread?" he thought.

And with that, the first sandwich was ordered.

What do you suppose was in the first sandwich? What sort of food might an English earl have kept in his castle two hundred years ago?

There probably would have been cheese, since nearly everyone ate a lot of cheese in those days. Only the very rich could afford to have meat like ham or beef or lamb every day. Most country people owned a few chickens and a cow, but these animals were kept alive in order to give eggs and milk. From the milk, people made yogurt, buttermilk, butter, and cheese.

The earl probably had some meat, since he could afford it. If he did, he probably also had salt with his sandwich. Before refrigerators were invented, meat was often salted heavily or smoked to keep it from spoiling.

Spices like mustard and pepper were very expensive, too. Many of them were brought all the way from Asia. It was while Columbus was looking for a quick way to sail to Asia for spices that he accidentally reached America, the home of the chili pepper and the tomato and other good things to put in sandwiches.

school

a place for learning

School Days 1895

Grand Rover Center School, where I went to school more than eighty years ago, was a painted wooden building. Inside was a big potbellied stove. On

wet days, we sat by the stove to dry our feet. The school had only one room, so all the grades were together. There was only one teacher to teach everybody.

Three kerosene lamps hung on each wall. They didn't give much light and always smoked. In the corner near the door was a bucket, a tin dipper, a wash pan, and a cake of soap in a tin can. There was one towel that had to last a week because washday came only on Monday. We had no well, so we carried water from a farmhouse half a mile away. It was a treat whenever Teacher sent me and my best friend for water. We petted the neighbors' cats while we took turns at the pump. The pail was carried between us, and we spilled at least half the water on the way back.

Children started school when their parents thought they were big enough. They quit when they were needed at home. The big boys came only in winter, because during the fall, crops had to be harvested and during the spring, the ground had to be plowed and planted.

At 9 A.M., Teacher rang her hand bell, and school began. We slid into our seats, smoothed our hair, and used our nose wipers (pieces of red dishtowels pinned to our dresses). In an emergency we used the ruffles in our petticoats. A boy's sleeve was the best he could do.

After we came to order, Teacher called the roll. We stood up and said, "Good morning, Teacher." We called all our teachers "Teacher."

After roll Teacher read to us. Then we would recite our lessons as we sat along the bench. The girls always left a

space so they wouldn't have to sit too close to a boy. While Teacher worked with the readers, an older student worked with us younger ones.

We learned the alphabet, how to count to ten, to print our names, and to read simple sentences such as "I see the cat. The cat sees me." To teach us the letters, Teacher printed words on our desks with chalk. Then we put kernels of corn on the lines. THE CAT

We learned to add by using toothpicks to make $| + ||| = ||||$

We took care of the few schoolbooks we had. They were handed down from year to year. There was a large dictionary at school for extra reading. In the front of the room was a map. It showed the United States on one side and the world on the other.

Discipline was important in a crowded one-room schoolhouse. We were taught at home to mind our elders, but we all acted up in school. We whispered, passed notes, and drew pictures instead of studying. Sometimes a boy at a desk behind one of us girls would dip one of our pigtails in the inkwell. The punishment for saying a dirty word was to have your mouth washed out with soap. For fighting, the big boys were whipped with a switch. Girls had their knuckles rapped with a ruler instead.

We each carried lunch in a tin pail and had a snack at recess. Beans piled on a molasses cookie was my favorite.

The last day of school was a day we liked. We slept the night before with our hair done up in rags so that we could have curls for the last-day-of-school program. We put on our Sunday best and wore hair ribbons. One year my chum Arilda Buck and I dressed alike in calico. We were very proud of our looks.

Our parents were invited to the program, and they came at noon with a picnic meal. We had chicken, potato salad, deviled eggs, beet and cucumber pickles, and big loaves of bread with butter and strawberry jam. We topped

popcorn. We were very disappointed when it was a card.

No one famous ever graduated from Grand Rover Center School, but that doesn't matter. It was still a good place to go.

After Vera Kurtz finished school, she became a teacher. She wrote this story of her school days for her great-grandchildren when she was eighty-five.

this off with four-layered frosted cakes. Afterwards Teacher gave us our report cards and a treat of either a pretty card or a snack of mixed candy, peanuts, and

skating

Stretch
Curve
Slant
Pant
Zooming
Faster
Shooting
Star

Swan
Spin
Whirl
Twirl
Graceful
Flowing
Dancing
Star

177

snake

a long, thin reptile with no legs

My Sister, the Snake, and I

My name is Cynthia Ann, but I am called Cindy. I am nine years old and have had this sister Emily all my life. She is twelve, and she is really silly. She is afraid of spiders, white mice, frogs, and snakes—especially snakes. But I think snakes are really great.

One day last summer, when I was visiting my aunt's and uncle's farm, I found a garter snake. I caught it to get a good, close-up look. It was as long as my arm and had three pale stripes and orange dots on its body. There were beautiful little blue slashes on its head. I

called it Red Eye because it had red eyes.

My uncle told me to take it home and keep it for a pet.

"No," I said, "Emily hates snakes. She's afraid of them."

"Nonsense," said my uncle. "Why would she be afraid of a little garter snake? It won't hurt anyone if it's handled properly."

"Oh, Emily wouldn't *touch* Red Eye," I said. "She'd scream and complain and carry on." Then I stopped. I remembered the time Emily had refused to lend me money for Dad's

178

birthday present. I thought of the time she had reported me for using her hairbrush to brush the dog.

"On second thought," I said, "she might learn a lot from Red Eye."

So my aunt gave me an empty coffee can, and I poked little holes in the plastic lid. (The holes were little ones because my aunt told me that snakes are escape artists and can get out of just about anything.) Then I took the garter snake home.

My mother helped me to find my old fish tank in the garage. It was just the thing for a snake.

I was right. Emily didn't like Red Eye. In fact, she hated that snake. But I loved it. I know it may sound funny, but whenever I came around the tank, Red Eye would rise up and stick out its long tongue at me, as if to say hello.

179

It was fascinating to watch Red Eye eat. When I put a piece of raw fish in the tank, it would open its mouth very wide and swallow the piece whole. Then for a day or two, you could see a large lump in Red Eye's body. The lump would get smaller and smaller as it went farther and farther down.

Before I got Red Eye, my sister and I didn't get along too well. After I got Red Eye, it was open warfare.

I was never allowed to tell about Red Eye's eating habits at dinner time. Emily said it made her sick. And once, when I brought the skin it had shed to the table, she started to scream.

"Do you have to let her bring that slimy skin to the table? I hate snakes! Hate them! Hate them!" she screamed. And she stormed out of the room.

"Snakes are not slimy," I yelled after her. I had just read a book called *Enjoy Your Snakes*, and I knew Emily was wrong.

But one day a terrible thing happened. I went into my room after school to say hello to Red Eye as usual. Right away I noticed that the top of the tank was slightly open. I thought maybe Red Eye had slid down under the gravel at the bottom of the tank. I stirred it around but saw nothing. Red Eye was gone!

"Mother," I screamed at the top of my voice. "Mother!"

Mother came running into the room. "What? Are you all right?"

"Somebody left the lid off the tank, and Red Eye's gone," I shouted.

"Oh, is that all?" Mother said thankfully. "You gave me a terrible scare."

"Is that all? Is that all? At this very moment Red Eye is wandering around somewhere. It could starve to death, or a dog could get it." I wanted to cry.

"Oh, come now, Cindy" said Mother. "We'll find Red Eye somewhere."

At that moment Emily came into the room.

"What's the matter?" she asked.

"You know what's the matter," I yelled at her. "You finally managed to get rid of Red Eye. I hope you're satisfied. I think you're a very mean person, and I hope Red Eye crawls into your bed tonight and scares you."

"I didn't do anything," Emily said. "I just got home from school."

I was not going to believe her.

"All right, girls," Mother said. "We'll all look for Red Eye."

"I'm not looking for any snake," Emily said with feeling.

I started to cry.

Emily looked at me in surprise. "You really like that snake, don't you?" she said.

"Of course," I sniffled. "What did you think?"

"I thought you were keeping it just to be mean—just because you know I hate snakes," said Emily.

I started to look for Red Eye. I didn't ever want to talk to my sister Emily again.

Emily watched Mother and me for a while, and then she sighed.

"Well, if that snake means that much to you, I guess I'll help you," Emily said.

We looked for hours—all over the house. I looked under the bed, in the sewing basket, in the ice-cream machine, behind the bookcase, and even in Mom's golf bag. I went through all the drawers in the desk. No Red Eye.

Finally Mother gave up. Emily came over and put her arm around my shoulders.

"I'm sorry, Cindy," she said. "I'm really sorry. We'll look after dinner. You can't give up yet."

Emily almost never touched me, except to poke me. It made me feel sad to think that she was really not a bad person, and that I had never known it.

182

But it made me even sadder that we couldn't find Red Eye. I sniffled all through dinner.

Mother, Father, and I were watching television later that night, when suddenly we heard the most awful screams coming from the bathroom. We

all went running in the direction of the noise, and there came Emily, running toward us. She was holding a bunched-up towel in front of her. Even when she saw us, she didn't stop screaming. But she dropped the towel, and out slid old Red Eye.

It took a while, but we finally got Emily calm enough to tell us what had happened. She had opened the closet door in the bathroom, and there was the garter snake, snuggled among the towels. When Red Eye saw her, it started to move. Emily knew that if she didn't grab the towel, it would get away.

After I got my snake back into the tank, safe and sound, I said to Emily, "Thanks for getting Red Eye for me."

She shuddered.

I knew it had been hard for her to touch a snake, and I knew she had only done it for me. But I didn't tell her that—I just gave her a hug.

When spring comes around, I'm going to put Red Eye in a coffee can. I am going to put on a plastic lid with small holes punched in it. Then I am going to take Red Eye back to my aunt's and uncle's farm and set it free. It will be safe and happy there, and it will never have to try to escape again.

It's the least I can do for Red Eye. And for Emily.

Woody says, "Let's *make* our soap.
It's easy.
We learned about it
In school."
He told Mother,
"All you do is
Take a barrel.
Bore holes in the sides,
And fill it with straw.
Ashes on top—"

"No," said Mother.

Soap-Making in 1750

squirrel

Squirrel has two meanings:

1. an animal with a bushy tail that lives in a tree
2. to collect something and keep it in a safe place

The squirrel will supply
a can of acorns.

Can Will squirrel a supply
of the acorns?

A Stick is a longish, thinnish piece of something, usually wood.

You can use a Stick to scratch with. There are two kinds of itches that are very hard to scratch. The first one is in the middle of your back. The second is when you have a cast on. The Stick for scratching under a cast has to be thin enough to fit between you and the cast. It is really terrible to have a cast on and not have a Stick to scratch with.

You can use a Stick for a lollipop, especially if the Stick is quite small. The same idea also works for popsicles and toffee apples. At grown-up parties, tiny pieces of cheese and little hot dogs have small Sticks stuck in them, which is really the same thing as a lollipop.

Maybe someday someone will invent a Stick that is tasty and good to eat. Then there will be much less to clean up after parties. Some people bury their used lollipop Sticks. They hope that the Sticks will grow into lollipop trees.

Sometimes a Stick is a magic Stick. Then it's called a magic wand. A wand is a thin and not very heavy Stick. It has to be light enough to wave around when casting spells. Some people claim that the magic is all in the person doing the magic, and that any old Stick will do. In any event, magic wands are very rare.

People who paint things are always stirring the paint with screwdrivers and kitchen spoons. They think that the paint will come off easily with paper towels. It doesn't. The best thing to stir paint with is a Stick.

A Stick also does a good job at stirring other things like soup and ice-cream sodas. At offices, people sometimes use little Sticks to stir their coffee.

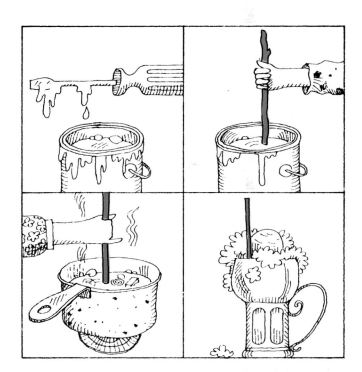

a Stick. The sign itself might be written on cardboard, which can be fastened to the Stick with staples or thumbtacks.

A baton is a thin Stick used by people who conduct musicians while they are making music. Most conductors use batons. A baton not only shows how fast the music should be played but also whether it should be loud or soft or happy or sad.

If you are carrying a sign, it is much better if you hold it up high with

If you have a trunk with a large lid, you will find that a Stick is very useful for propping it open. A Stick is also helpful in propping up 1) hoods on cars, 2) windows, 3) trunk lids on cars, 4) trapdoors, and 5) clotheslines.

People who have apple trees often use Sticks to prop up the tree branches. If they didn't, a branch might break off from the weight of all the fruit growing on it.

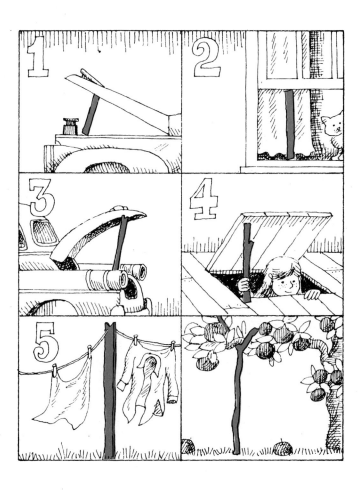

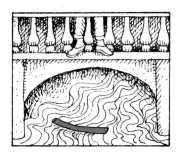

Because nearly every Stick floats, it is useful for throwing into rivers (and streams). Throw a Stick off a bridge over a river (or stream), and then run to the other side of the bridge and wait for the Stick to come out. When it does come out, you have some idea how fast the water is flowing.

If the Stick does not come out, there are several possibilities. Perhaps your Stick was extra heavy and sank. (But not many Sticks sink.) Perhaps the river (or stream) was flowing the other way. Maybe your Stick has gotten stuck or has been stolen, perhaps by a beaver or somebody under the bridge.

Dogs love to fetch things, and most people like to throw things for dogs to fetch. A Stick is just about the best thing for a dog to fetch. It is the right shape and size to fit across a dog's mouth, like a bone. But it is better than

a bone, because a dog might not want to give the bone back to the thrower. And besides, it doesn't matter very much if the Stick gets lost where the dog can't find it.

You will probably not be able to go camping without a Stick. You can use one for holding up your tent, for holding a pot over a campfire, for toasting marshmallows, and so on.

One obvious way to use a Stick is to see how deep things are. When service station attendants check the oil in car engines, they do it with a dipStick. When you are in deep snow, you can see how deep it is with a Stick. And with a Stick you can see if a river is shallow enough to walk across or deep enough to drive a boat along.

If you are lucky enough to have Two Sticks, there are, of course, many more things you can do. But perhaps the best thing is to use just one Stick and keep the other one as a spare.

A Stick is good for poking into places where you'd rather not put your hand.

sun

Oh sun, a plea:
Send down your heat
upon the peas to
make them sweet.
Oh sun, a plea:
Your heat will mean
that beans will grow
long, thin, and green.
Oh sun, oh please:
Without your heat
to make the peas and beans grow green,
We won't have food to eat.

The sun is stuck.
I mean, it won't move.
I mean it's hot, man, and we need a red-hot
poker to pry it loose,
Give it a good shove and roll it across
the sky
And make it go down
So we can be cool,
Man.

Myra Cohn Livingston

193

Have you ever stepped on a rock that has been sitting in the sun for a long time? If you were barefoot— OUCH! What made the rock hot was solar energy. Heat from the sun was stored in the rock.

Of course, the rock will get cool again after the sun goes down. But it will take a while. The rock will stay warm longer than the air will.

Today, people are trying to learn ways to store heat from the sun and

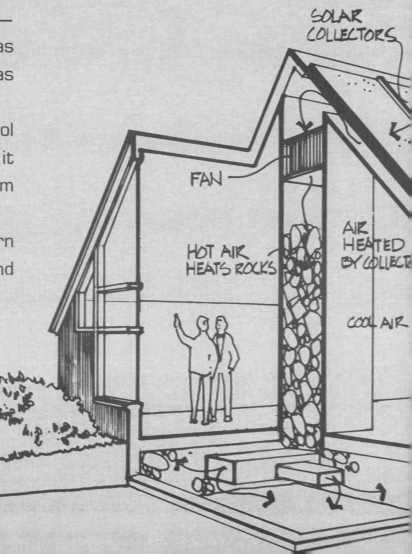

SOLAR COLLECTORS

FAN

HOT AIR HEATS ROCKS

AIR HEATED BY COLLECT

COOL AIR

use it to heat houses. If enough of the sun's heat can be saved, people can keep their houses warm at night and on cloudy days, as well as on sunny days.

The first step is to collect the sun's heat. A solar-heated house usually has large glass panels on the roof. These are called collectors. The sun shines on the collectors all day, and they get hotter and hotter.

Then air or water runs inside the collectors and gets hot, too. The hot air or water is piped to the storage area. The hot pipes heat up rocks in the storage area. Rocks will hold the heat for a long time and release it very slowly. The heat from the rocks can keep the house warm at night. Most houses still need regular furnaces in case the sun does not shine for several days.

Two bicyclists are slowly pedaling along, one behind the other. A man in a car drives by. He offers the second bicyclist ten dollars if she can pass her friend. The first bicyclist doesn't speed up. But the second bicyclist can never ride past her. Why not?

Turn to page 334 for the answer.

tease

Sometimes
when I'm teased
I don't cry,
I go away.
When I come back
they're doing something else.
I remember.
They forget.

197

tile

a thin piece of clay, stone, or wood

cut out. It is also easy to fit squares and rectangles together tightly, because their sides are straight. When tiles cover a thing perfectly, the pattern that they make is called a tessellation. The word

Tiles are used to cover all sorts of flat things like floors and walls and roofs. Most ordinary tiles are square or rectangular. That's because squares and rectangles are easy shapes to measure and

tessellation comes from the Latin word *tessella*, which means "a little square." Little squares make up many kinds of tessellations. But not all tessellations are made with tiles. Checkerboards,

fit together well, too. Triangles make good tessellations. In fact, the shapes in a tessellation can be very strange, just as long as you can fit them together perfectly. Can you make one?

checkered shirts, some patchwork quilts, and fancy floors are all tessellations, because they are made up of little squares.

Tessellations can be made up of other shapes that

tingle-airy

Melvin: What is a **tingle-airy**?

Clara: A **tingle-airy** is a hand organ played on the street. It is often decorated with **piddock** shells.

Melvin: What are **piddocks**?

Clara: **Piddocks** are little animals that make holes in rocks, in wood, and in the walls of **gazebos.**

Melvin: What is a **gazebo**?

Clara: A **gazebo** is a round building with windows. From the windows you can often see **cotoneasters**.

ting′gəl - er ē   pid′dok   gə zē′ bō

Melvin: What are **cotoneasters**?

Clara: A **cotoneaster** is a flowering bush. It is a favorite of **mumruffins**.

Melvin: What is a **mumruffin**?

Clara: A **mumruffin** is a bird. It often visits bird feeders in winter to eat **pobbies**.

Melvin: What are **pobbies**?

Clara: **Pobbies** are small pieces of bread **thrumbled** up with milk and fed to birds and baby animals.

Melvin: What is **thrumbled**?

kə tō′nē as′tər   pob′ēz
mum′ruf ən   thrum′ bəld

201

Clara: **Thrumbled** is squashed together. Crowds in streets **thrumble gongoozlers.**

Melvin: What is a **gongoozler**?

Clara: A **gongoozler** is the kind of person who always stops on the street to look at a **tingle-airy**.

gon güz′lər   ting′gəl - er ē

too

Too means "also." There are other words that sound the same but are spelled differently. Can you tell what they mean?

203

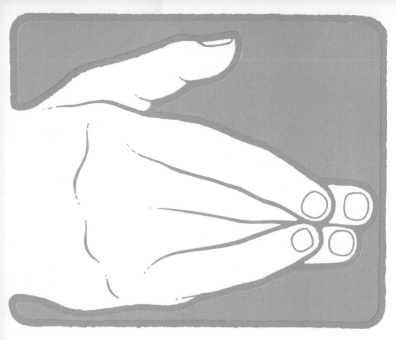

toughie

a hard thing to do

Two Touching Toughies

1. Try to touch your little finger and your index finger together like the fingers in the first picture.

2. Look straight ahead. Then slowly raise your arms over your head and touch the tips of your index fingers together without looking at them. Next, try to touch them behind your back. Then close your eyes and try to bring your fingers together in front of you.

treasure

something very valuable

Nearly two hundred years ago, in 1795, three boys beached their canoe on a small island in Canada called Oak Island. Then they went exploring. On a hill near the shore, they saw a strange old oak tree. In the bottom branch were deeply cut grooves, perhaps made by a heavy rope. Beneath the branch was a round dip in the ground. It looked as if someone had dug a hole there once.

To the boys, all these clues could mean only one thing—*buried treasure!* Something heavy must have been

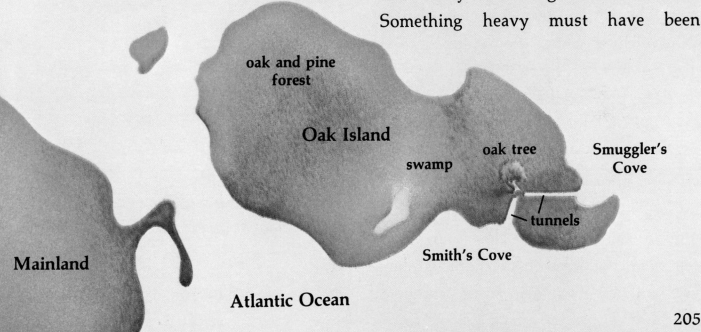

oak and pine forest

Oak Island

swamp

oak tree

Smuggler's Cove

tunnels

Smith's Cove

Mainland

Atlantic Ocean

lowered into a hole by a rope wrapped around the branch. Perhaps pirates had buried a chest full of golden coins or jewels beneath the tree!

The next day the boys returned to the hill with shovels and picks. They dug down ten feet and hit something hard. A pirate's chest? No. It was only a rough platform made of wooden planks. Day after day the boys dug. Every ten feet they found more wooden planks. When winter came, they stopped their digging, but not their investigating.

The boys spoke to old-timers about Oak Island. The old-timers said that the island was jinxed. Fifty years before, strange ships had anchored there. Eerie noises sounded across the bay. One night fishermen rowed close enough to see people huddled in the light of roaring bonfires. Two men went ashore to find out what was happening. They were never seen again. After listening to the old-timers, the boys were certain that a treasure must be on the island.

Years later, one of the boys raised enough money to search again for the treasure. He bought a winch and a block and tackle. He hired workers to

help with the digging. As they dug deeper, they found layers of coconut mats and charcoal. At ninety feet they discovered a new clue. It was a flat stone three feet long and one and one-half feet wide. The stone was covered with strange writing.

Although the treasure hunters did not know what the writing meant, they were excited by the discovery. The workers dug rapidly. When they had dug down ninety-seven feet, they struck wood again. Surely they were close to the treasure! But it was nearly dark, and they stopped work. The next morning, they found the hole filled with salt water. They bailed and pumped for weeks, but the water filled the pit faster than the workers could empty it.

The next summer, the treasure hunters dug in another spot. But at 110 feet they hit water again. There would be no treasure discovered there.

The search was abandoned until forty years later. This time the treasure hunters used a horse-powered drill.

They hoped to find out what was below the surface in spite of the water. When they brought the drill up, three pieces of gold chains were caught in the machine. Now they must be near the treasure! If only they could drain all the water from the hole!

Where was the water coming from? The workers searched the island and discovered a hidden tunnel that drained water from the Atlantic Ocean into the treasure pit. It seemed that someone had built the tunnel to hide the treasure with water. No matter how the diggers tried, they could not keep the water out of the treasure hole.

In 1893 a group of people formed the Oak Island Treasure Company. They used a steam drill to search for the treasure. The drill brought up a tiny ball of parchment. On the parchment were a

"w" and an "i" written in black ink. A little bone whistle carved like a violin was discovered, too. Perhaps the pirates who hid the treasure had dropped these things.

But the water still kept the treasure hunters from personally going down to search for the treasure. At last in 1897 they gave up.

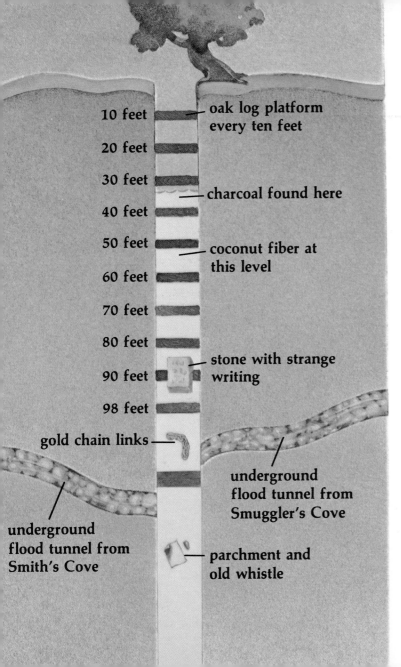

10 feet — oak log platform every ten feet

20 feet

30 feet — charcoal found here

40 feet

50 feet — coconut fiber at this level

60 feet

70 feet

80 feet

90 feet — stone with strange writing

98 feet

gold chain links

underground flood tunnel from Smith's Cove

underground flood tunnel from Smuggler's Cove

parchment and old whistle

Others tried, too. In 1909 Franklin Roosevelt, who later became president of the United States, looked for the treasure with his friends. But they had no luck either.

Since the search began nearly two hundred years ago, people have spent over two million dollars looking for the Oak Island treasure. One man even lowered an underwater TV camera into the hole. He was sure he saw three treasure chests. But even with modern machines, all the searching has failed to find the treasure and to answer the questions about it.

Who built the underground tunnels?
How did they do it?
Who thought of this grand puzzle?
Where did the treasure come from?
And most important—what is the
    treasure?

tree

trouble

Something that's easy to get into but hard to get out of

try

The Creek

Nine-year-old Kelly O'Brien inched his way home from school. Folded inside one of his books was his monthly report card. It showed the same marks as the last one. After two months of special classes, Kelly had shown "no progress." And progress was what his parents wanted. Without it, Kelly knew that he was in trouble!

Mother's car was not in the driveway. Kelly found his sister Shannon in the kitchen.

"Where's Mom?" he asked.

Shannon shrugged.

"I'll be at the creek," Kelly said.

"You had better do your exercises," Shannon said in a sassy voice.

Kelly ignored her and went outside. Walking across the grass, he tripped. It made Kelly cross. His feet were clumsy, his hands were clumsy, and he was clumsy inside his head. He couldn't even play ball because his feet got mixed up when he tried to run and think at the same time.

The exercises were supposed to help him get over his clumsiness, but they weren't helping. He was sick of them.

At the end of the back yard, Kelly climbed down a small bluff to the creek and dropped into his boat. Grabbing the paddle, he pushed against the mud. At low tide there was more pushing than paddling.

To make the creek safe for Kelly, Mr. O'Brien had fenced off both ends. Kelly mud-poled his way to the fence near the marsh, hoping to find Phillip there. Phillip was his only friend now that all the kids were playing ball.

"Phillip? Phillip?" Kelly called.

Phillip was a biology student at college. He was doing a nature study in the marshy creek. Since the two had met in the marsh a few weeks ago, Phillip had taught Kelly the scientific names of the plants and animals there.

"Phillip!" Kelly called again.

"Ho!" came Phillip's answering cry.

On the bank just beyond the fence gate was an area that Phillip had staked off with sticks and string. Stepping onto the bank, Kelly sank halfway to his knees in mud. He laughed and didn't mind at all. It made him feel like Phillip, who was mud-caked to his knees every time Kelly saw him.

"I've made some more sketches," Phillip said. He kept records in a notebook.

Kelly admired people who could draw. He couldn't draw a circle or a square or even the letters of the alphabet, much less a fiddler crab. He had been told it was something about mixed-up signals between his brain and his eyes, hands, and feet.

"What kind of crab is this?" Phillip asked, picking up a fiddler crab.

213

"A blue mud fiddler, *Uca pugnax*," Kelly answered.

"Good boy, Kelly," Phillip said. "I wish I had known as much about the creek when I was nine years old."

Kelly grinned with pleasure.

"Away from this marsh," Kelly thought, "people think I'm dumb. But here, I'm smart enough."

"Kelly! Kelly!" It was Shannon's voice, calling him.

"Coming," he hollered. "That's my sister," he said to Phillip. "I have to go now."

As Kelly ran into the house, Dad called, "Hi, sport! Been playing a tough game of ball?"

Kelly looked down at himself. He was muddy, as if he'd been playing something rough. He grinned, thinking how pleased his father would be if he thought Kelly liked to play football.

"Well . . . uh," Kelly mumbled.

"I'm glad you're learning to play ball," Dad said. Kelly shrugged and went to clean up.

At the dinner table, Kelly's mother said, "Your sister saw you down at the marsh with a man, Kelly."

"That's right," Shannon said. "And

the man was barefooted, had no shirt, and had the bushiest hair I've ever seen."

"In the marsh?" Dad asked. "I thought you said you were playing ball this afternoon."

"Dad, I'm no good at stuff like that," Kelly said. Whew! He had gotten it all out.

"You never will be good at it till you try, will you, sport?" Dad said.

"Speaking of trying . . ." Mother said. "Your monthly progress report doesn't show any change at all."

"You're going to have to work really hard," Dad continued. "I think one thing you need, Kelly, is a set of rules about the creek. You spend far too much time there."

Kelly stared at his plate. Didn't they know that he was smart at the creek? Unfortunately, "creek" wasn't on his progress report.

"And I'd like a daily progress report from school," Mother added.

Kelly groaned.

"And now, about this man in the marsh," his mother went on. "You know we don't like you talking with strangers."

"Phillip is not a stranger, Mom." Kelly put down his fork. "He goes to college, and he is doing a nature study in the marsh."

"I don't like the sound of it," Dad said, "talking with strangers—"

"But . . ." Kelly began. Then he sighed and turned away. He knew he could never win the argument.

"Yes, sir," he said quietly.

After supper Mother handed Kelly pieces of heavy cardboard with shapes cut out of them. They were the same shapes his teacher gave him at school. There were circles, squares, and triangles. Kelly took the circle in his left hand and began tracing the shape with his right finger.

"Round," he said as he traced the circle.

The exercises were supposed to train his hands to work with his brain. Kelly had been doing the exercises for two months, but he still couldn't draw a good, round circle or a square with sharp corners.

The next day in class, Kelly was fidgeting at his desk.

"If you can't do your work, you can at least be still and quiet," Mrs. Jordan and his parents always said.

"Be still," Kelly told himself. Being still took every bit of his energy.

"I don't get it," Kelly thought. "Here at school I can't sit still. But at the creek I can be as still as a rock. I like to sit quietly, watching the crabs."

A voice broke into Kelly's thoughts.

"I wonder if Kelly can answer that question for us?" It was Mrs. Jordan, and she was talking to him.

Kelly blinked. What question? He had been so busy being still that he hadn't heard any question. He knew that the teacher didn't mean to embarrass him. She had promised to call on him only when she thought he knew an answer.

"Well, I don't think Kelly can help us this time," Mrs. Jordan said. "But isn't Kelly behaving nicely today?"

Everyone nodded. Kelly grinned.

"Smash you all," he thought.

When Kelly got home from school

that afternoon, his mother met him at the door. "Did you have a good day?" she asked.

"Yup," Kelly said, handing her the teacher's note.

"Hmm," said Mother as she read the note. "Mrs. Jordan doesn't say you had a good day. You're still not trying, Kelly."

"Not trying?" he thought. "How do you measure trying?" Out loud he said, "I *am* trying, Mom."

"Not hard enough, Kelly. No more creek until your teacher feels that you are trying," Mother said firmly.

"Yes, ma'am," Kelly said sadly.

He walked into the living room and slumped into a chair. But the creek pulled him like a magnet. Kelly moved to the window and looked out. He couldn't see the creek from there. Before

Kelly knew what he was doing, he pulled the door open and ran to the creek.

An empty ice-cream carton had washed into the marsh near the fence. It was one of the big kind that he had seen at the ice-cream shop. Kelly fished the

carton toward him. It reminded him of the circles he traced—a perfect round "O."

"Round," he said aloud.

"Round," echoed a voice. It was Phillip. "What are you doing there?"

Kelly wanted to grin and tell Phillip he was just playing, but he could never fake with Phillip. He shrugged and said, "Exercises for dumb people. I'm dumb, Phillip!" Kelly shouted. "I'm dumb all over."

"Hey! Come here!" Phillip called.

But Kelly was running up the bluff. The one place where Kelly felt smart and knew he was smart was at the creek with Phillip. Now it was ruined because of those dumb exercises.

His mother was standing at the top of the bluff. Before Kelly was up, she reached out and grabbed him.

"You were not only in the creek," she said, "but talking to that stranger. Up to the house, young man."

Kelly glanced back. Phillip was standing there, watching.

Kelly stumbled all the way to the house. His mother took him to his room and closed the door behind him.

"Don't come out until I say so," she said.

Kelly couldn't remember ever seeing her look so angry. She didn't seem like the same person who rubbed his head or read to him. Was it his fault that letters looked different from one time to the next? The *d*'s and *p*'s kept turning upside-down and backward. Could he help that?

Stupid circles, anyway. He walked over and kicked a dent in the rim of his waste basket. Picking up the waste

219

basket, Kelly rubbed his hand around the rim. It was crooked now, like the circles he drew. His hand didn't travel smoothly around the rim. It bumped across the bent part. Kelly turned the basket upside-down. He rubbed the bottom rim that wasn't bent.

"Round," he said slowly. He smiled. He was beginning to feel the roundness. Putting the waste basket down, he sat at his desk and drew circles with a pencil. Suddenly he grinned. A perfect circle!

Kelly forgot why he was in his room. He had to share his joy. Grabbing the paper, he ran out the door.

"Mom! Look!" Kelly shouted as he bounded down the stairs.

"I told you to stay in your room," she said, coming around the corner. She whirled him around and sent him back.

Kelly left the paper on the stairs and ran into his room. He threw himself on the bed.

Minutes later Kelly heard his mother calling to his father, "Come look at this!" And then his parents were in his room, hugging him and rubbing his hair and patting his back as if he'd scored sixteen touchdowns. Later, after all the excitement, Kelly rolled over and fell asleep.

The sound of talking woke him. He listened. That was Phillip's voice!

Quietly, Kelly got up and tiptoed to the door. What was Phillip doing here? What was he telling his mother? Opening the door, Kelly sneaked down the stairs. Carefully he peeped around the corner. Phillip happened to be looking at the exact spot where Kelly's head appeared.

"Ho, kid!" Phillip called across the room. "I came to see if everything was O.K."

"Phillip and I have been talking," Mother said. "He's helped me to understand some things."

"He has?" Kelly asked. "What things?"

"I think that you should tell your class about the marsh," Phillip said.

"Huh?" said Kelly.

"About fiddlers, for instance," Phillip explained.

Kelly shrugged and rolled his eyes. He would really feel stupid telling people about fiddlers. "Everybody knows about fiddlers," he said.

Phillip laughed. "Some people don't notice what's right in front of their noses. Mrs. O'Brien, can Kelly come with me now to gather specimens at the creek?"

"All right," Kelly's mother said, smiling.

The next day Mrs. Jordan was happy to see that Kelly had brought something to share with the class. Kelly held a jar tightly as he walked to the front of the room.

"Aw, it's just fiddler crabs," someone said, groaning.

"It's two different kinds of fiddlers," Kelly began. "There are mud fiddlers and sand fiddlers. The scientific names for them are *Uca pugnax* and *Uca pugilator.*"

"Huh?" said one kid.

"Oh, sure, Kelly," said another.

"Yeah, sure," Kelly said loudly. "The mud fiddler is *Uca pugnax* and the sand fiddler is *Uca pugilator*. I have a male and female of each," he said. "See their claws? The crabs make waving motions with their claws when they fight. It looks as if they were playing the fiddle. That's why they're called fiddler crabs. On the male crabs one of the claws is very big. If the big claw

breaks off, another regular-size claw grows in its place. Then the other claw grows into a big one.

"The males eat with the small front claw. The females use both front claws to eat. First they take mud into their mouths. They don't eat the mud, but they eat things out of the mud. Then they spit the mud into a claw and set it aside. That's what makes those funny little droodles you see wherever there are fiddlers."

Kelly hardly stopped to take a breath.

"The blue mud fiddler, the *Uca pugnax*, is darker than the sand fiddler, to match the mud. See the blue spot between its eyes?"

Half the students left their desks and crowded around for a look. "Let me see, let me see," they said.

"Well, Kelly," Mrs. Jordan said, when he had finished, "that was excellent."

After school Kelly ran all the way home, carrying his daily report.

"Mom! Mom!" he yelled as he came in the doorway. "I have a good report today! I know I do."

"I should say so," she said, smiling.

"Mom, can I . . . can I, please?" Kelly asked.

"All right. You can go to the creek," she said. "But be home in time for supper."

Kelly ran outside and down to the creek. He pushed the boat into the water.

"Phillip!" Kelly called. "Phillip!" he called again.

And then Kelly heard the answering "Ho!"

If ewes use yews
And you use ewes and yews,
Who uses a "U"?
You or a ewe or a yew?

224

umbrella

Through the window
I see the soft rain.

Through the soft rain
I see the neighbor's fence.

And just above the fence
I see fully opened umbrellas
Softly flowing from left to right
On and on.

Hidden by the neighbor's fence
I cannot see
Who goes there
Under each of the umbrellas.

But, I see each umbrella
Softly flowing from left to right
On and on,
Shading the someone under it
In the soft morning rain.

umpteen

a large number

A Dime's Worth for Free

It wasn't that Billy hated arithmetic so much. It was just awfully hard to concentrate on the first really hot day of spring. The windows were open, and the weather coming in made everybody just itch to get outside.

But Mr. Dowd didn't understand. When he collected the arithmetic tests, he nearly had a fit. Practically all the answers were different, and all of them were wrong.

That's when he gave the class a lecture. He said that if this was the best they could do, perhaps they needed a good arithmetic drill. Then he filled the blackboard with numbers. Everyone

had to copy them down, add them up, and turn the answers in by tomorrow morning.

At three o'clock, Billy and his next-door neighbor Chris left school gloomily. The sun was still hot, and the warm breeze still smelled of wet dirt and new

leaves. But the whole day was ruined.

"It'll take two hours to do all that homework," Chris said.

"Two! It'll take three, at least! There are umpteen problems here," groaned Billy. He folded his homework paper as small as possible and stuck it in his pocket. Just then his fingers found a dime he had forgotten about. When Billy showed the dime to Chris, she cheered up a little.

"Say, let's go down to Menton's and get a dime's worth of jellybeans," Chris suggested.

"Or some dill pickles. I could eat umpteen pickles," Billy said.

"Jellybeans," said Chris, who had a real sweet tooth.

Menton's store was cool and dark and smelled of salami, cinnamon, and new magazines.

"Well, now, what can I do for you?" asked Mr. Menton, as he always did.

Billy and Chris were still arguing about dill pickles and jellybeans when the phone rang. After a minute, Billy and Chris quit arguing and began to listen.

"What? What?" shouted Mr. Menton. He looked very upset. Finally he slammed the phone down.

"What's the matter?" Billy asked

"Emil!" snapped Mr. Menton. Emil was his nephew who drove the delivery truck. "Just wait until I see him! He parked in front of a fireplug. Now he and the truck have been taken down to the police station. So I have to go pay the fine to get him out. There's no one to make deliveries and no one to mind the store."

It was then that Billy got his bright idea. "Look, Mr. Menton," he said, "we'll mind the store. Won't we, Chris? We know the price of just about everything."

"I don't know," said Mr. Menton, looking at Chris and then at the soft drink cooler and then back at Chris again. He knew all about Chris's sweet tooth. "Well, all right. But don't eat anything while I'm gone, and when I get back I'll give you a dime's worth for free. O.K.?"

"Sure," said Chris and Billy.

Mr. Menton hurried off. As soon as he was gone, Billy headed straight for the cash register.

"What are you doing?" asked Chris, looking shocked.

"We've got to hurry. Mr. Menton will be back any minute," Billy said.

Chris turned pale. "Have you gone crazy?" she asked. "What are you doing with that cash register?"

"Homework. We've got umpteen problems to do, don't we?" said Billy, getting out his list of numbers. "Look here. You just punch the keys for each number and then punch "total." The answer jumps right up. You can add all umpteen numbers at once. See?"

Chris said, "Hot diggity! But it all comes out dollars and cents."

Billy was already punching away. "That doesn't matter." He punched "total." A bell rang, and $89.92 jumped up in the register. Then the cash drawer shot out and punched Billy in the stomach.

"Ouch!" he yelled. But Billy forgot about the pain as he copied down the answer to the first homework problem—8,992.

"Let me do the next one," said Chris, standing back a safe distance from the cash drawer.

Chris worked several problems. Then Billy took a turn again. Chris began to think about what she would get with her dime's worth for free. She took the lid off the soft-drink cooler. No raspberry pop. She dragged a couple of empty boxes to the back of the store, so that she could stand on top of them to see if there was any more raspberry pop.

Meanwhile Billy was ringing up the last problem. Just then a man walked in. Billy punched "total." The bell rang, and the cash drawer popped out.

"Leave it open, kid!" said the man in a gruff voice. "This is a stick-up."

It was just like in the movies. The man reached for the money.

"Hey! You can't do that. Mr. Menton won't like it." Billy's voice was shaking. "Chris!" he shouted.

Chris was nervously balanced on a pile of boxes with a bottle of raspberry pop in each hand. When she heard her name yelled out, she jumped. The boxes shifted, and Chris let go of one bottle to hold on to the shelf.

The bottle hit the cement floor and exploded. Chris yelled and dropped the other bottle. It exploded, too.

The man shouted, "Drop that gun! I've got you covered."

This was too much. Chris lost her balance completely and came tumbling down with umpteen bottles. The explosions sounded like a machine gun.

The hold-up man headed for the door just as Mr. Menton, Emil, and Officer Grier walked in.

"Stop that man!" yelled Billy.

Officer Grier grabbed the hold-up man, and Billy rushed to explain.

Right then, Chris staggered up to the front of the store. Her shirt was all red, and red drops dripped from her hair and the tips of her fingers.

"Get a doctor! She's bleeding!" cried Mr. Menton.

"Am I?" asked Chris. She licked her fingers. "No. It's just raspberry pop."

After Officer Grier took the robber away, Billy and Chris began to explain. In the end even Mr. Menton wasn't too upset, although the store was a mess.

"Hey, how does it feel to be a hero?" whispered Billy to Chris.

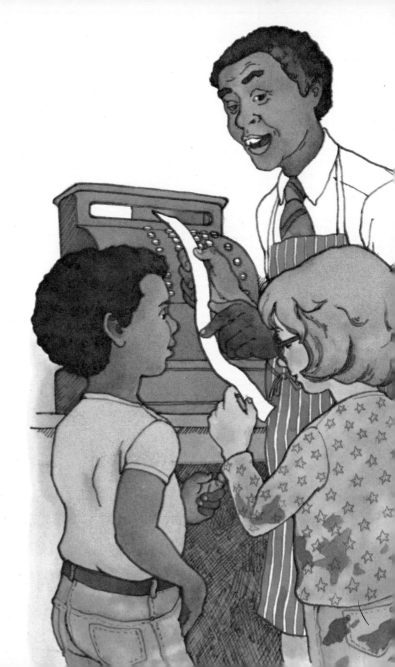

But just then Chris remembered the dime's worth for free.

Unfortunately, as they were trying to make up their minds—dill pickles or jellybeans—Mr. Menton began to examine the cash register.

"It looks as if you did an awful lot of business today, kids. To be exact— $6,948.73," said Mr. Menton.

Billy and Chris looked puzzled.

"Look," said Mr. Menton. He pointed to the cash register. "Every time I make a sale, I ring it up here. At the end of the day, I pull this handle and push the "grand total" button. Then the register shows how much money I've taken in all day."

"Oh-oh," said Chris.

Billy looked at his shoes.

"And then," Mr. Menton continued, "I count the money in the drawer. It's supposed to come out the same as the register total. But something fishy has been going on here!"

Well, then it all came out. Billy explained about the homework and his bright idea.

"Oh, sir," Billy said, squirming, "I never knew the cash register kept a total of all the numbers."

Chris and Billy were beginning to feel less and less like heroes.

"It certainly does," said Mr. Menton. "Now, how am I going to find out how much money I ought to have in the cash register?" Mr. Menton looked at Chris and Billy. They just shrugged.

"There is just one way," Mr. Menton continued. "You two take that homework paper and add together all the answers to all the problems. Then you can subtract that answer from the total on the cash register."

"$6,948.73?" asked Billy and Chris.

"That's right—$6,948.73," said Mr. Menton.

He handed them each a pencil and a piece of paper.

"Hey, how does it feel to be a hero?" whispered Chris to Billy.

Billy just groaned.

understanding

unfortunately

without luck

Noses

"There, there,"
said the old lady
tweaking my nose

I

unfortunately

couldn't reach hers

unicorn

a make-believe animal

ady Margaret had commanded Lord Jeffrey to prove his love by bringing her a unicorn's horn. Lady Margaret had just been teasing, but Lord Jeffrey did not know that. Eager to please, Lord Jeffrey had ridden in search of the wild beast. But that had been two months ago. No one had heard from the loyal knight since then.

Lady Margaret sat sadly in her castle. She hated herself for letting Lord Jeffrey go on the quest. If anything happened to him, she would never forgive herself. Even Glenda, her lady-in-waiting, had little hope.

"Ah, my lady, I fear Lord Jeffrey will never come back," said Glenda. "You know the legend of the unicorn. Only a young maiden can capture the wild beast. The maiden need only call, and the lovely unicorn will

236

come gently to her side. But a knight! The unicorn will attack him with its dangerously sharp and pointed horn!"

Just then there was a clatter of hoofbeats in the courtyard.

"It must be Lord Jeffrey!" cried Lady Margaret, running to the window.

In less than a moment, Lord Jeffrey was at Lady Margaret's feet. He knelt before her, kissing her outstretched hand.

"Speak not, dearest lady, before I give you proof of my love," he said. "I bring you the gift you asked for."

Lady Margaret watched in amazement as two servants entered, bearing a long, twisted ivory horn. Lady Margaret laughed with joy as they placed the gift at her feet.

"This is the proof you wanted, my lady," Lord Jeffrey proudly said. "I fought the cruel knights who

guarded the Enchanted Forest. For days I wandered, searching in vain for the unicorn. At last, as I rested hopelessly by a pool, the wild beast appeared. A great horn grew in the middle of its sleek, white forehead. The twisted horn gleamed in the glittering sunlight. Silently, I crept towards the unicorn. As it bent its proud, silken head to drink, I lifted my sword. With one swift blow, I cut off its horn. The beast was furious. But without its horn, the unicorn could not do battle.''

"Ah, my noble knight,'' sighed Lady Margaret.

And they lived happily ever after.

What Lady Margaret didn't know (and you can be sure Lord Jeffrey never told her) was that he had bought the horn from a merchant in a distant town.

What Lord Jeffrey didn't know (and you can be sure the merchant never told him) was that the horn did not come from a unicorn at all. In fact, it was not really a horn. It was a twisted tusk from a small whale called a narwhal.

You see, the merchant couldn't give Lord Jeffrey a real unicorn's horn because there was no such animal.

Why did Lady Margaret, Lord Jeffrey, and maybe even the merchant believe in unicorns?

Well . . . long, long ago, before there were books or cameras, people told stories and drew pictures of strange animals that they had seen. But because the drawings weren't perfect and the stories were told differently each time, the real animals became more and more difficult to recognize. Slowly, a rhinoceros became a beautiful white horse with a long, twisted horn like a narwhal's. And the name that people gave to this wonderful beast was the unicorn.

United States of America

No matter where you go in the United States, you're bound to find something special happening. Here are a few of the special events that you might see around the country.

1. Jumping Frog Jubilee
2. Unicycle Invitational
3. Indian Wild Horse Rodeo
4. Luling Watermelon Thump
5. Old Timers' Skiing Derby
6. Circleville Pumpkin Show
7. National Hollerin' Contest
8. International Pancake Race
9. Abbott's Magic Get-Together
10. National Jousting Tournament
11. World Championship Chili Cook-Off
12. World Championship Cornstalk Shoot
13. International Worm-Fiddling Contest
14. National Wild Turkey Calling Contest
15. National Oldtime Fiddling Contest and Festival

19. Peru Circus Festival
20. Choctaw Indian Fair
21. The Omak Stampede
22. Turkey-Rama

16. Hobo Convention
17. Moab Jeep Safari
18. Annual Turtle Trot

Peru, Indiana, was once the headquarters for five great American circuses. Today it's the home of the annual Peru Circus Festival, with a parade and big-top show in which all the performers are kids. The kids are picked from the schools of Peru. They are trained for two months by experienced circus performers who live in the town.

Before the telephone was invented, the people who lived near Spivey's Corner, North Carolina, used to

keep in touch with each other by hollering across the valleys. Now every year they hold a National Hollerin' Contest, with hollerin' and callin' events for men, women, and children.

worms come out of their holes. Whoever catches the most worms in the shortest time is the winner.

The Jumping Frog Jubilee takes place every May in Angels Camp, California. You just bring your frog and set it down on the launch pad. Each frog has thirty seconds to take its first jump. The winning frog is the one that jumps the farthest. If you didn't bring a frog, you can still rent one at the jubilee's rent-a-frog booth.

Another special contest is the International Worm-Fiddling Contest at Careyville, Florida. Worm fiddling is an old way to catch worms for fishing. You hammer a wooden stick into the ground. Then you rub the stick so that it vibrates. The vibrations in the ground make

Colon, Michigan, is a town of magic. For one week each year, the whole town is turned into a fantastic magic show during Abbott's Magic Get-Together. Magicians from across the country perform tricks on all the street corners, pulling rabbits out of hats and making things disappear.

unmarked

not labeled

The Puzzle of the Unmarked Crossroads

Pretend you are on a hike to Mudville. You leave your hometown early in the morning. After walking for a few hours, you reach a spot where two roads cross. The signpost has been knocked over and is lying on its side. You do not know which road goes to Mudville. But suddenly you think of something that will help you find your way.

How can you tell which road goes to Mudville? For the answer see page 334.

244

unusual

extraordinary

A Walk on an Iceberg

On summer afternoons, under our orchard trees in Maine, Grandmother told us stories. The best ones were the true stories about her own life. Our favorite was about the day Grandmother took a walk on an iceberg. Every time we heard the story, shivers ran up and down our spines.

Grandmother would always tell the story in the same way. If we thought she was going to leave something out, we would all interrupt to remind her.

It all began in 1860, when my grandmother married a young sea captain. Many wives waited at home for their husbands to return from the sea.

But it never occurred to Grandmother to stay at home. Whenever Grandfather went to sea, she went with him.

"Now, one spring morning," Grandmother would always begin, "your grandfather and I spotted an iceberg as big as an island."

"That iceberg is just right for a walk," my grandmother told my grandfather. "It's so big and sunny that I'm sure it's quite safe. And one side slopes gently down to the water and looks just right for a landing."

"No iceberg is safe for a walk," Grandfather said. "Just put that idea straight out of your head."

"I'll do no such thing," said Grandmother. "I'll stick by you through thick and thin. But that doesn't mean I'll always do as you say. You might as well get used to that idea right now."

So with my grandfather fretting and frowning and worrying, Grandmother went with three sailors and a young scientist named Kemper Swift to explore the great iceberg. Soon they were on it, clambering up its side.

"My word!" Kemper Swift said, as he looked around. The iceberg was so enormous that there were flocks of seagulls on it and herds of seals.

"Poor beasts!" Kemper Swift said. "I wonder where they'll go when the iceberg breaks up, if it ever does."

When Grandmother got to this part of the story, we would always interrupt.

"Get along quickly, Grandmother!" my brother John used to say. "It isn't gulls or seals we want to hear about. We want to hear the good part."

"I'm coming to it," my grandmother would say. "I won't forget. No! Surely I never shall. For just then," she would exclaim, "we saw a man!

"At first we couldn't believe our eyes! Still, there he was, a real man alone on that iceberg! He was so scared to see us that he ran away. He was in rags and tatters and so thin that his very bones stuck out."

"Don't forget a word about what he looked like!" my brother John would interrupt.

"I won't," she said. "His legs were just like sticks. His face was covered with whiskers, and his hair fell down over an old, ragged red coat he had on."

"Don't forget his eyes or his nose

or the way he kept falling down," I would say.

"Just give me time," Grandmother said. "His eyes looked like great burnt holes in his poor face. They were full of terror, as though he were seeing ghosts. His nose was like a sharp knife. And he kept falling down like a lot of toothpicks."

"Don't forget his language!" my sister Edith would cry.

"I won't forget a single thing," Grandmother answered. "The three sailors ran and grabbed him. They said it was just like trying to hold on to a lot of sharp bones. They asked him who he was and what he was doing on the iceberg. But he only screamed strange words.

"Then Kemper Swift bent over the poor man and began to talk to him in what seemed to be a dozen different languages. I thought that I had never heard so many strange sounds coming out of anyone's mouth."

"Now's the time you always tell us that we should learn languages," my sister Edith said.

"I'm going to, right now," my grandmother said. "I won't forget that, for it is most important. When you children grow up and go away to schools, you must learn languages. It's wrong to know only your own language and no other at all. There isn't one chance in ten million that you'll ever walk on an iceberg the way I did. But you might well meet someone who can't speak a word that you can understand, and you would miss a chance to know that person. So you must learn any other language you can. Now don't forget!"

"Go on about Kemper Swift!" my brother John begged.

"I'm coming to him," my grandmother said. "Kemper Swift discovered that this poor man could understand German."

"And then you found out how he got on the iceberg," John cried.

"Yes. But whose story is this, I'd like to know?" Grandmother teased.

"The man said he had been out on the ice, hunting a few miles from his cabin. But when he started back, what did he find but a sea of water between him and the land! That great sheet of ice had just broken away from the land, and he was caught like a prisoner!"

We always shivered even though we sat in the hot summer sun when Grandmother said these words.

"Finish the story, Grandmother," we begged.

"Well," she said, "the three sailors gathered up the man like a bundle of sticks and took him down to our boat. And our walk on that iceberg ended right then and there. For we all wanted to take that poor man to our ship and give him hot food, fresh water, and a good, warm bed. And that's just what we did.

"When your grandfather saw us coming, he just couldn't believe his eyes. Then he gave orders to set sail to Germany, so that we could take the man home. And that's my story."

"But is it all true, Grandmother?" we asked.

Then she always said, "Every word of it is true. Just as true as your hands are. Just as true as your feet are. Just as true as those trees above your heads."

ups and downs

Life is full of little ups and downs.

251

V

Sometimes I see them,
The South-going Canada geese,
At evening, coming down
In pink light, over the pond, in great,
Loose, always dissolving V's. . . .

vanish

disappear

Cover a glass of water with a hat. Then say to your buddy, "I bet I can drink all the water in that glass without touching the hat."

Take a pencil. Put one end to your lips and the other end to the hat. Then say, "It's simple with this magic straw."

Pretend to drink the water through the magic straw. Then say, "The water has vanished!"

When your buddy lifts the hat to see if it's true, you simply pick up the glass and drink the water without ever touching the hat.

variation

a different way of doing something

"Little Red Riding Hood" is a story that has been told many different times and in many different ways. Here are two variations.

A Little Red Riding Hood Poem

There was a little girl who was very, very good.
She was known all around as Red Riding Hood.
(The reason, of course, that she had such a name
Was the cloak that she wore—it was always the same.)

One day Mother asked her, "Please be a dear
And take food to your Grandma, who can't come here."
(The reason, of course, that Red Riding Hood would go
Was that Grandma told stories that were fun to know.)

She dashed through the woods in a very good mood,
With a smile on her face and a basket of food.
(The reason, of course, that her speed was so great
Was that Grandma would worry if she were late.)

Then a wolf popped out from behind a tree
And said, "Please stop and have a chat with me."
(The reason, of course, that the wolf was so sweet
Was that Red Riding Hood would be a tasty treat.)

Red Riding Hood said no, and then she hurried by.
The wolf nodded slyly and winked his wicked eye.
(The reason, of course, that the wolf wasn't mean
Was that he could reach Grandma's without being seen.)

When Red Riding Hood arrived, she raced to Grandma's bed.
But she spoke not a word—she stopped and stared instead.
(The reason, of course, for Red Riding Hood's fright
Was that Grandma was surely a fierce-looking sight.)

"Your teeth are so big, and your nose is so long,
And your ears are so furry—something is wrong!"
(The reason, of course, for Grandma's strange face
Was that the wolf had taken Grandma's place.)

A woodcutter came in and killed the wicked beast,
Grandma was saved, and they all had a feast.
(The reason, of course, for all the laughter
Was that now they would all live happily ever after.)

A Little Red Riding Hood Play

Wolf:
(to audience)

I've had it! For years I've been taking the blame for what happened to that Red Riding Hood brat. Well, it's about time someone heard my side of the story. It all began one morning in the woods. . . .

Red Riding Hood:

Get out of my way, you grubby mutt!

Wolf:

I'm sorry if I'm in your way. Where are you going this fine day?

Red Riding Hood:
(walking away)

I'm going to my grandma's! What's it to you, you dirty old dog?

Wolf:
(to audience)

Well, needless to say I felt it my duty to warn Mrs. Hood, the poor soul, that her rude little granddaughter was on her way over. So I hurried down a short cut I knew.

257

(*Knock, knock.*) Mmm. No answer. The poor woman is probably hard of hearing. I'll just take a peek. (*He walks into the house.*) Why, what's this? A note! I'll read it.

> Dear Red,
>   I've married the woodcutter, and we've gone to the seashore on our honeymoon.
>   Toodle-oo,
>   Granny

Red Riding Hood: (*Knock, knock.*) Open up, Granny! I don't have all day!

Wolf:
(*jumping into bed*) Oh, dear! If she finds me here, she'll think I ate her grandmother. I'd better disguise myself—and quickly. Where's that nightcap?

Red Riding Hood:
(*opening door*) What's happening? Are you still lying around in bed? Why, you have the biggest ears I've ever seen.

Wolf: Well . . . er . . . well . . . the better to hear you with, my dear.

Red Riding Hood: *(suspiciously)*	What about those gigantic eyes?
Wolf:	Ah . . . er . . . the better to see you with, my dear.
Red Riding Hood:	And what about those big, sharp fangs?
Wolf:	The . . . ah . . . er . . . the better to eat the goodies you brought in that basket, dearie.
Red Riding Hood: *(clubbing wolf with the basket)*	Oh, yeah? You're not my grandmother. You can't fool me. You're the wolf! Take that, you flea-bitten cur!
Wolf: *(to audience)*	With that, the horrid little girl started throwing the goodies from her basket at me. I had to defend myself, didn't I? So I ate her. It was the only thing I could do. What would you have done in my place?

259

VARLET

villain, rascal, scoundrel, ruffian, rapscallion, rogue, scamp, stinker

V. Vinnie Valiant (the V stands for Virgil) was traveling on his new velocipede to a seaside village for his vacation.

"Why, look!" V. Vinnie Valiant said. "On the veranda! It's Vicky Vigglestein."

And indeed it was. Vicky Vigglestein was on the veranda playing her violin while watching the vivid view in her violet velvet gown.

Just then that vicious varlet Vernon Viper appeared on the veranda. He removed a vial of the most deadly venom from his valise.

"So, Vicky refused to be my valentine, did she?" Vernon Viper sneered. "I'll poison her vermicelli!"

But just in the nick of time, V. Vinnie Valiant switched vials and replaced the deadly venom with vitamins.

261

"Now my victim will be very sorry!"
said that villain Vernon Viper. But he
was mistaken.

For with just one bite of the vitamin-
enriched vermicelli, Vicky was full of
vim, verve, and vigor.
"Take that, you vile varlet!" Vicky said,
and she whacked Vernon very vigor-
ously on the head with her violin.

262

vegetable

How can you change a pumpkin into another vegetable?
Throw it up in the air, and it will come down squash.

What's purple and goes slam slam slam slam?
A four-door cabbage.

What's red and goes putt-putt-putt?
An outboard tomato.

What's orange and glows?
An electric carrot.

What's green and writes?
A ballpoint cucumber.

What did the string beans say to each other?
Nothing. Beans can't talk.

What's green, then white, then green, then white?
Broccoli that works nights as cauliflower.

venture

a risky thing to do

Just Another Rainy Day

Saturday it rained. My father asked me if I'd like to go to the movies.

"Just me?" I asked.

"No, all three of us," he said. "You, me, and Fudge."

Fudge is my brother, Farley Dexter Hatcher. He's three years old.

"Fudge is too young to go," I said.

"Oh, I don't know, Peter," said my father. "He seems old enough to me."

I could tell that Dad had made up his mind. But it sounded like a risky venture to me. (That's what my teacher always calls it when somebody has a bright idea that isn't so bright.) Still, a movie was a movie.

"What'll we see, Dad?" I asked.

My father checked his *New York* magazine. "*A Bear's Life* is playing in the neighborhood," he said. "How does that sound?"

"What's it about?" I asked.

"A bear's life, I guess," my father said. "It's rated G."

I was thinking of a good western with lots of action. But my father had already made up his mind. *A Bear's Life* it would be.

By one o'clock we were ready to go. All three of us wore our raincoats and boots, and my father took his big black umbrella. The movie theater wasn't very far away. My father said the walk would do us all good. It was really pouring, so there were a lot of puddles.

I jumped over the puddles, and my father went around them. But not Fudge—he jumped right into every one and splashed around like a little duck. By the time we got to the movie theater, the legs of his pants were soaked. My father stuffed a bunch of paper towels up each pant leg so Fudge wouldn't have to sit there with wet legs. At first Fudge complained, but when my father bought him a big box of popcorn, he forgot about his stuffed pants.

Right after we got settled in our seats, a big boy sat down in front of Fudge, so he had to change seats with my father. Now Fudge was on the aisle,

I was in the middle, and my father was on my other side.

When the lights dimmed, Fudge said, "Ohh . . . dark."

I told him, "Be quiet. You can't talk in the movies."

"O.K., Peter," he said.

I guess that's when he started throwing his popcorn. At first I didn't notice, but I wondered why the people in front of us were turning around every second to peer at us. Then I heard Fudge whisper, "Pow-pow-pow!" and I saw him throw a handful of popcorn.

I poked my father. "He's throwing his popcorn," I whispered.

My father reached across me and tapped Fudge on the leg. "If you throw one more piece, I'm going to take it away from you."

"No throw," Fudge said loudly.

"Shush," the people in front of us said.

"Shush!" Fudge said back to them.

"You see?" I told my father. "He's too young for the movies. He doesn't understand."

But from the moment the first bear

came on the screen, Fudge sat still and watched. After a while I forgot all about him and concentrated on the movie. It was much better than I thought it would be. It showed lots of bear cubs and how they live.

I'm not sure when I realized that Fudge was gone. I guess it was when I turned to ask him if he had any popcorn left. I had already finished mine and was still hungry. I was really surprised to see that he wasn't there. I mean, one minute he was sitting right next to me, and the next minute he was gone.

"Hey, Dad," I whispered to my father. "He's gone."

"What?" my father said.

"Fudge isn't in his seat."

My father looked over. "Where did he go?"

"I don't know. I just noticed he was gone."

"Let me out, Peter. I'll find him," he said.

I stood up to let my father out.

A few minutes later the picture stopped—right in the middle of a scene. The sound track trailed off, and all the lights came on. The audience let out a groan. Some kids called, "Boo . . . boo!"

Then my father and two ushers and the theater manager came over to me. "He was sitting right here," my father told them, pointing to the empty seat on the aisle.

"Well," the theater manager said, "we've checked the restrooms and the office. And we know he's not behind the candy counter. We'll just have to search the theater." The manager cupped her hands around her mouth and shouted, "Ladies and gentlemen . . . may I have your attention please? We'll continue with our film in one moment. But first we have to find a three-year-old boy who answers to the name of Fudge."

Some people laughed when the manager said the name. I guess *Fudge* does sound funny if you're not used to it. I thought, "Maybe he's been kidnaped!" Then I thought, "Who'd want to kidnap him, anyway?"

"What should I do, Dad?" I asked.

"Why don't you walk up and down this aisle and call him, Peter?"

"O.K." I said.

"Here, Fudge," I called, starting down my aisle. I sounded as if I were calling a dog. "Come on out, Fudge."

When I got down to the first row and called, "Here, Fudge," he popped out at me. He scared me so much, I yelled, "Ooooh!"

"Hi, Peter," he said.

"Hey . . . I found him," I called. "I found him. I found him. Here he is!" Then I turned to my brother. "You troublemaker! What are you doing way down here? And why are you sitting on the floor?"

"I wanted to touch the bears," Fudge said, "but bears are all gone." He spread out his arms. "All gone."

My father and the ushers and the theater manager ran to us.

"Fudge," my father said, scooping him up, "are you all right?"

"He wanted to pet the bears," I said. "Can you beat that?"

"Well, I guess we can continue with the picture now," the theater manager said. She cupped her hands

268

around her mouth again and said, "Thank you, ladies and gentlemen. Our young man has been found safe and sound. Now we return to the conclusion of *A Bear's Life.*"

Later, when we got home, my father tried to explain to Fudge that movies are like TV. "Those are just pictures on a screen," he said. "There are no animals to touch."

Fudge listened, but Dad knew that he didn't really understand. He still thought those bears were in the theater somewhere.

Dad winked at me, and I knew what he meant. Taking Fudge to the movies had turned out to be a risky venture, all right. And we wouldn't do it again—at least not until he was a lot older.

veterinarian

an animal doctor

I was just finishing my breakfast when I heard a horn beeping outside. A truck had stopped in front of my house. The driver announced that he had a sokomoto for sale. In his language, *sokomoto* meant a chimpanzee.

I expected to see a small chimp in the back of the truck, but instead the chimpanzee was enormous! It was the biggest sokomoto I had ever seen. It was sitting wrapped inside folds and folds of heavy hunting net.

"For just six dollars, it's yours. A very low price," the man said.

I started to say no. What would I do with a chimp? But then I noticed that the chimp's right hand was badly hurt.

270

"How did that happen?" I asked the driver.

He shrugged. "Some hunters caught it in the bush a few days ago. They were looking for antelope, and they saw a band of chimpanzees in the trees. A branch cracked, and this sokomoto fell and knocked itself out. The hunters wrapped it in a net. Then, while they were carrying it home, the chimp woke up. I guess it was really frightened and wanted to get loose. It stuck its hand through the net and caught one of the men by the arm. The hunter was startled. He hit the sokomoto with a knife to make it let go."

"Why didn't anyone take care of the poor animal?" I asked angrily. "Can't you see its wound is badly infected? The chimp might die."

"Well, why else do you think I'd sell a chimp for

only six dollars?" the driver replied. "No one knew what to do for the wound. Besides, the sokomoto wouldn't let anyone come near. I said I'd try to sell it."

The situation was clear. If I didn't buy the chimp, it would probably die.

I shrugged and gave the driver six dollars. He helped me unload the heavy bundle from the back of the truck. We carried the chimp to the garage. Then the man drove off. I was glad to see him go.

I went back to the garage. I locked the door from the inside and picked up a sharp knife.

The chimp was a young male. He was smaller than I, but he looked very strong. Even with his wounded hand, he could probably break most of my bones if he wanted to.

The young sokomoto followed my every move with his big brown eyes. I decided to take a chance and cut him free. I knew that young chimps are very affectionate. They love to be played with, talked to, and hugged. So I began by giving the chimp a name. I called him Joseph. I spoke gently and calmly.

All the time I smiled at Joseph, for I knew that chimps smile at each other to show they are friendly. I spoke to Joseph for about ten minutes, pointing to the net and knife. Joseph listened carefully. He looked at me with pleading eyes and strained at the net. Finally I gave Joseph a pat on the head and a big kiss on the nose. The chimp hooted with happy surprise.

First I cut the net away from Joseph's right hand. I looked at the wound closely. It was even worse than I had thought. Joseph winced with pain as I touched his hand. But he did not pull away. So I freed Joseph's legs, watching him carefully. He didn't move. Then I started to cut through the layers of net wrapped around his body.

Joseph remained quiet. All that was left were the ropes around his arms. Carefully I cut the ropes.

Now the net lay in a circle at Joseph's feet. He was free. But he remained completely still for a few minutes. Finally, pushing his lips forward as far as they would go, he hooted and then smiled.

I hooted back at him and smiled, too. He stared at

me intently. Then he moved toward me slowly. His face looked sad. He raised his hurt hand and looked at it. I held out my hand. Very carefully Joseph rested his swollen fingers on my palm. Then he let out a long "Ooooooh."

I looked at his hand carefully. Joseph watched me. He hooted softly. He seemed to understand what I was doing.

Everything was fine until I tried to leave the garage. Then the chimp ran after me, crying like a baby. I led Joseph back to his corner and sat down opposite him.

"Stay here!" I said loudly, holding one finger up to his nose. But as soon as I got up to leave, Joseph tried to follow. I pushed him back, and we both sat down again. And again. And again for more than an hour. Then finally he decided to stay in the corner. I left in a hurry, locking the door from outside. Joseph began to cry very, very sadly. I tried not to listen as I ran to the jeep.

Quickly I drove to the veterinarian's, but she was

away. Her assistant gave me some medicine and lots of bandages. I would have to be the chimp's veterinarian. I hurried home as fast as I could.

When I returned to the garage, Joseph was waiting near the door. He scrambled to his corner and sat down. He remained quiet, even when I washed his hand. And I knew how it must hurt!

Joseph looked at his hand. He held it very close to his eyes. He turned it slowly from side to side. Then he put his hand back in mine.

When the wound was clean, I put some medicine on it. Then I wrapped the hand in an extra-long bandage, for animals usually try to chew bandages off.

Later that evening I brought Joseph some food. The bandage was still on his hand. But it was red with blood. I changed the bandage while Joseph nibbled on some crackers and a banana.

It was getting late. It had been a hard day for both of us. But when I tried to leave, Joseph surprised me. He followed me, took my hand, and pulled me back into his corner. I sat down, wondering what he

wanted. Joseph sat down next to me. He grunted happily and leaned heavily against my side.

Nothing happened for a long while, and I started to fall asleep. I woke up with a start when something tickled my chin. Quietly and very carefully, Joseph was examining my face with his fingers. He pulled my lips out to look at my teeth. When he tried to pinch my nose, I snorted loudly.

By then Joseph was getting sleepy. His head nodded, and slowly he rested it against me. Then he put his unhurt hand on my knee. He held it there, waiting. So I took Joseph's hand in my own, and we fell asleep.

victory

Myra Cohn Livingston

a successful struggle

Hey, this little kid gets roller skates.
She puts them on.
She stands up and almost
drops over backwards.
She sticks out a foot like
she's going somewhere and
falls down and
smacks her hand. She
grabs hold of a step to get up and
sticks out the other foot and
slides about six inches and
falls and
skins her knee.

      And then, you know what?
She brushes off the dirt and the
blood and puts some
spit on it and then
sticks out the other foot

        again.

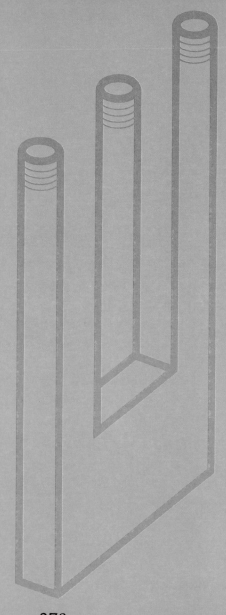

What's wrong with this widget?

wallpaper

It took Bill Wall 27 days to wallpaper one wall. When asked why it took so long, Wall replied, "A wall well papered is a wall Wall done."

wapiti

wap i ti (wop'ə tē)
A large North American deer. Also called "elk," "American elk."

There goes the Wapiti, Hippity-hoppity!

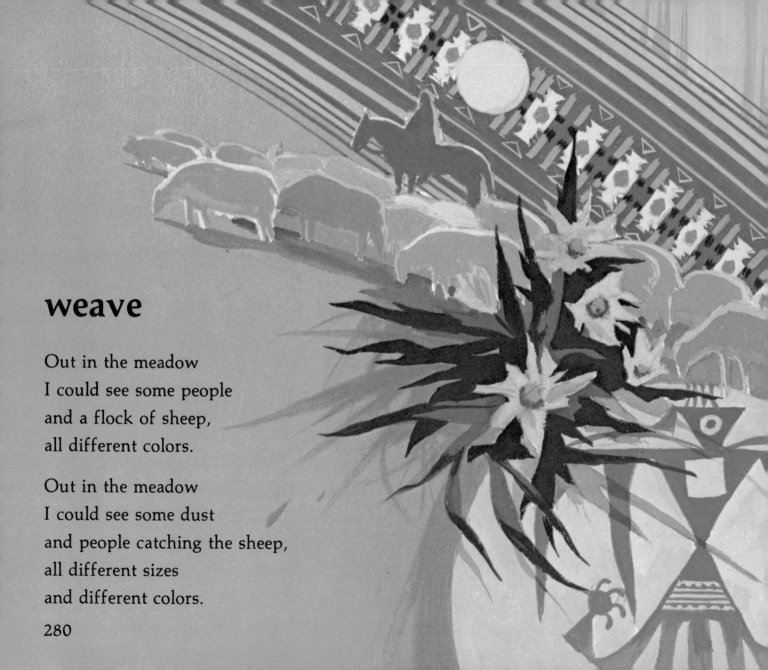

weave

Out in the meadow
I could see some people
and a flock of sheep,
all different colors.

Out in the meadow
I could see some dust
and people catching the sheep,
all different sizes
and different colors.

280

Out in the meadow
I could see some people
shearing that pretty wool
off those beautiful colored sheep.

Out in the meadow
I could see some people
with big brown bags.
Within the bag
I could tell there was wool
off those beautiful colored sheep.

281

Out in the meadow
I could see some people
washing that pretty wool
from those beautiful colored sheep.

Out in the meadow
I could see some wool
lying out in the sun
to be dried
and in the sun
the wool was dried.

Out in the meadow
I could see some people
carding that pretty wool
and I could see
some starting to spin
that pretty wool.

Out in the meadow
I could see some people
starting a big loom
and they started to dye
some of that pretty wool.

Out in the meadow
I could only see
an Indian girl
with long black hair
starting her first time
weaving a rug.

window

Windows are a building's eyes. People inside look out through them, and the world outside looks in. *Window* comes from the Old Norse word *vind-auga*, and that means "wind-eye." They were called wind-eyes because they let fresh air in and looked like eyes in the house. Wind-eyes also let in the sunshine and let out the smoke from the cooking fire before chimneys were invented.

To keep out snow and rain and cold air, the earliest windows had simple curtains, which were called window-panes. (*Pane* comes from the Latin word for rag.) Later, when people discovered how to make glass, they began to use it for their window-panes. Sometimes they used glass of different colors to make beautiful pictures and patterns for the sunlight to shine through.

wish

Meg stood beside her brother Frank, waiting for the bus to Grant City. Meg didn't want the bus to come, but she knew it would anyway, so she wished it would hurry up. At last she saw the bus coming down the dusty road. Meg fought down a scratchy feeling in her throat. For the second time that morning, she felt she was going to be sick.

Frank looked down at her and said, "Remember, Meg. If you are too unhappy, you can come back to Bow Junction."

Meg nodded.

"But give your new home a good try," he added. "Don't give up too soon. Promise."

Before Meg could promise anything, the bus rolled to a stop.

Frank gave Meg a kiss, and a smiling bus driver reached out to help her board the bus.

"I'll put your carryall in the overhead rack," he said.

"Thank you," said Meg.

"How are you today?" the driver asked.

Meg ignored the question and said, "I'm going to Grant City."

"Yes, I know you are," answered the driver.

"I'm going to live with my aunt and uncle," she continued. "My brother says I have to because he can't take care of me and the farm, too."

"That sounds reasonable," said the driver.

"He says that I was a big help on

the farm when Mom was alive. But now that she's gone, I'm too much trouble."

"He said that?" the driver asked.

"Well, it wasn't exactly like that," admitted Meg. "But that's what he meant."

"Well, the city isn't such a bad place," said the driver kindly. "Once you get settled and make some friends, I'm sure you will like it."

"I doubt it," answered Meg.

Meg looked out the window at her brother as the bus lurched and rumbled onto the road. Frank waved, and she waved. Then the bus picked up speed, and Meg couldn't see Frank anymore. As she watched the tiny town of Bow Junction slip past, she felt as if everything she had ever known was slipping away from her.

Meg sat up straight in the seat. She

closed her eyes, crossed her fingers, and made a wish. She felt that it was the most important wish of her life. "I wish I'll be home again soon," she thought. "I wish, I wish, I wish."

Five hours later, the bus pulled into the busy Grant City station. As the driver helped Meg off the bus, she glanced at all the strangers crowding the platform. She didn't see anyone familiar. But Uncle Peter spotted her almost immediately.

"Megan!" he shouted. "Hello! Did you have a good trip?"

"I slept some," she answered shyly. "It was long."

"We'll be home in just a minute," Uncle Peter promised. Then he turned and yelled, "Taxi!"

When they arrived at the house in Union Square, Aunt Paulette was at the door. She gave Meg a hug and said, "Welcome to your new home."

Aunt Paulette had fixed a special supper, but Meg wasn't hungry. And no one knew quite what to talk about.

Aunt Paulette finally cleared the table and said, "You must be very tired, Meg."

"No," she lied, "I feel great."

"Don't you want to see your new bedroom?" asked Uncle Peter.

"Sure," Meg lied again. She did not want to go to bed. She did not want to be left alone in a strange room. But she knew she would have to go sooner or later.

Aunt Paulette led her upstairs to the third-floor bedroom. "Uncle Peter and I are very glad to have you here, Meg. We hope you will be happy."

Meg didn't know what to say, so she said nothing. She began digging into her carryall for her toothbrush. Aunt Paulette waited for Meg to smile or say something. Finally she kissed her niece goodnight and left.

Meg dropped the toothbrush and went digging again into her carryall. There was the white envelope. Inside was a return ticket to Bow Junction. There was also a note from Frank.

Dear Meg,
Keep this return ticket until you are sure you will be happy. Then cash it in and buy yourself something nice.

Love,
Frank

Meg stared at the note for a long time. Then her eyes swelled with tears of anger.

"I will never be happy here," she blurted out loud. "Never, never! And I'll never cash in the ticket, either! I'll keep it to go back to Bow Junction."

Meg put the ticket back in the envelope and made herself a promise. She would stay long enough to satisfy the grownups. Then she would use her ticket to go home.

Downstairs in the kitchen, Uncle Peter and Aunt Paulette were talking. "Stop worrying, Paulette. Megan will be fine in a few days," Uncle Peter said. "We all agreed that bringing her here was the wisest decision."

"I know, I know," answered Aunt Paulette. "But children don't always understand. She looks so unhappy."

Uncle Peter picked up the empty cups and walked to the sink. "Give her time," he said gently. "Give her time."

The next morning, Meg sat on the front steps and stared at the strange new neighborhood with its tall, crowded houses. School wouldn't start for two more weeks. What could she do until then?

"Hey, girl!" Meg heard someone yell. "Catch that skateboard!"

Meg looked up and saw a yellow board streaking toward the steps. She jumped up, grabbed it, and turned to face whoever had yelled. It was a girl her own age. She had plastic bandages on both knees, and her head was covered with tiny braids.

"Hi!" said Meg. "My name is Megan."

"Mine's Cally," said the girl.

"Cally! What kind of name is that?" asked Meg.

"It's my kind of name," answered Cally. "What's wrong with it?"

"It's a nice name," said Meg. "It's just different."

"Well, I am different," said Cally. "And I'm the best skateboarder in the whole city."

"So what's a skateboarder?" asked Meg, looking puzzled.

Cally stared in disbelief. "Where have you been, girl? Don't you know anything?"

"I've been in Bow Junction," Meg answered hotly. "I rode horses and worked on the farm with my brother. I didn't have time for silly games."

The two girls glared at each other. After a few dangerous seconds, Cally relaxed. She rolled her skateboard back and forth with her foot and asked, "Are you going to stay here for long?"

Meg relaxed too and answered, "I'm staying until Thanksgiving."

"Well," said Cally, "that's a long time away. Do you want to be friends till then?"

"Sure," said Meg. "Will you show me how to fix my hair like yours?"

Cally reached out and touched Meg's fine red hair. "Can't do that," she said. "You've got the wrong kind of hair. But I'll teach you how to skateboard."

"I guess I'd like that," agreed Meg.

That night, Meg looked at her return ticket to Bow Junction. She had surprised herself when she told Cally that she was staying until Thanksgiving. The idea had just popped into her head. But now, after thinking about it, she decided that it was a good idea. "People always go home for Thanksgiving," she told herself.

Besides, there was another, better reason for going home then. Frank's birthday was right before Thanksgiving. Meg wouldn't dream of missing her brother's birthday. So it was decided. When Thanksgiving came, she would go home.

The next two weeks raced by. Meg and Aunt Paulette shopped for school clothes and a skateboard. Every afternoon Meg and Cally practiced skateboarding in the park down the street. The two girls became good friends.

On the first day of school, Meg was delighted to discover that she and Cally were in the same class. All the kids liked Cally. And soon Meg had a lot of friends, too. Each day, Meg went to school and afterwards played with her new friends. But each night, when she was alone, she would take out her bus ticket and say, "Hurry up, Thanksgiving. Hurry, hurry!"

Then came October, and Cally announced that she was going to enter the City Skateboard Championship for Girls.

"It's on October twenty-seventh," she told Meg. "You can enter too, but you're going to have to work hard. The competition will be tough."

"Sure," answered Meg. "I like tough competition."

Cally was a good teacher, and so Meg already rode a skateboard with skill. But during the next three weeks, Cally was more than a teacher. She was a drill sergeant. She demanded that Meg practice every afternoon. She set up difficult obstacle courses, and Meg learned to weave in and out of orange markers set only inches apart. Cally also taught Meg how to jump obstacles that stood above ground and to land on her moving board without losing her balance.

Cally practiced more difficult tricks like flips, handstands, and spins.

By the end of the second week, both girls were patched with plastic bandages. And every night Meg fell into bed, exhausted.

When October twenty-seventh arrived, all the hard work paid off. Out of eighty-four contestants, only fifteen were chosen for final competition; and out of those fifteen, Cally took first prize, and Meg tied for sixth. The day was a triumph!

"Well," said Meg after it was all over, "what shall we do now?"

"Oh, next month we'll be plenty busy with rehearsals," answered Cally.

"Rehearsals for what?" asked Meg.

"For the Thanksgiving play," answered Cally. "The third grade puts on a play for the whole school every Thanksgiving Eve. The parents come. It's a big event."

Meg's eyes lit up. "What part are you going to play?" she asked.

"Oh, one of the Indian chiefs, I guess. They get the best lines. What part will you try for?" Cally asked.

Meg didn't know what parts there were, but she tried to think of something impressive. It was always hard to impress Cally. Then suddenly she remembered something she hadn't thought of in weeks. Her face turned serious, and she said, "I can't be anything. I won't be in the play."

"Why not?" asked Cally in surprise. "Everybody is." And then Cally remembered, too. "Oh yeah," she said sadly, "I forgot. You're going home."

Meg nodded.

"Well, you could change your mind, couldn't you?" asked Cally. "Maybe at the last minute, you'll decide not to go."

Meg shrugged. "All the parts will be taken by then," she said.

"Well, you could be a turkey," said Cally hopefully. "There are always lots of turkeys, and all they have to say is gobble gobble."

Meg almost laughed, but she just

shook her head. "No," she said. "I don't think I will change my mind."

Suddenly Cally clenched her fists and glared at Meg. "Why do you have to go? Tell me that, girl. You don't have to go. I know you don't have to go. What's so special about Bow Junction?"

For a second Meg couldn't think of an answer. Then she said weakly, "Bow Junction is my home. I miss my brother . . . and friends . . . and horses and, and chickens and . . ."

"Horses! Chickens!" shouted Cally. "What are you saying? Here I am, your best friend! We've done everything together! I helped you in the skateboard championship! And all you care about are some old horses! Well, Megan Casey, we are not friends anymore. I'm through with you, girl. You are the selfishest person I know."

With that, Cally turned and ran.

Meg was stunned. She stared until Cally was out of sight. In a daze she walked home.

"Megan," said Aunt Paulette, "what's the matter? Are you sick?"

"Cally and I had a fight," Meg answered, still in a daze.

"A fight about what?" asked Aunt Paulette.

Meg did not look at her aunt. She hadn't told Aunt Paulette about her Thanksgiving plans. She wasn't sure this was the best time to do so.

Finally she answered, "Cally's mad because I won't be in the school play."

"That doesn't sound like Cally," said Aunt Paulette. "There must be something else. And why won't you be in the play?"

Meg bit her lip, then blurted, "Because I'm going home!" And she burst into tears.

Aunt Paulette took Meg in her arms. "But you are home, Megan," she said.

"No!" sobbed the girl. "Fra-Fra-Frank gave m-me a ticket. And it's his bir-bir-birthday!"

Meg's chest felt as if it were full of sharp rocks. She couldn't breathe, and she couldn't stop crying. Aunt Paulette held her and said nothing.

Then, when Meg finally controlled her tears, Aunt Paulette said, "I know about the ticket, Meg. It was Frank's way of saying he still loves you. But he was sure you would be happy here. And we all thought you were happy. Aren't you?"

Meg answered, "I was. I am. But— but— "

"Well," said Aunt Paulette, "if you really want to leave, perhaps you should leave right away."

Meg thought for a moment and then said quietly, "But I love you and Uncle Peter. I don't want to leave. Not anymore. But it's too late. Cally won't be my friend. She says I'm selfish."

Aunt Paulette gave Meg a handkerchief and made her blow her nose. Then she said, "You're not selfish, Meg. You're just stubborn. Once you get an idea in your head, you can't let go of it. Find Cally and tell her you have changed your mind."

Meg shook her head.

"Just try," said Aunt Paulette. "See what happens."

Meg didn't have to look far. Cally was sitting on Meg's front steps. And she looked almost as miserable as Meg.

"I'm not leaving," Meg said simply.

Cally looked up.

"And I'm going to be in the play," Meg added.

A slow grin spread across Cally's face. "Gobble, gobble?" she said.

"Gobble, gobble!" answered Meg.

Thanksgiving came quickly. The play was a big success. Meg played a Pilgrim, and she had six whole lines to say. But Cally stole the show. She dropped a pumpkin, and it splattered all over the Indian chiefs.

Uncle Peter and Aunt Paulette came to the play. Frank came too, all the way from Bow Junction, and stayed for the holiday.

As soon as they got home after the play, Meg ran to her closet. She got out a very long, thin package.

"Here," she said to Frank. "This is your birthday present. Was it ever hard to wrap! Happy birthday."

A grin spread over Frank's face as he unwrapped a fishing rod. "Hey, Meg! This is just the kind I've been wishing for. But where did you get the money? You must have been saving for months."

"Oh," Meg answered casually, "I cashed in an old bus ticket that I'd been saving. I decided I wouldn't need it after all." She gave Frank a hug.

"And I got my wish, too," Meg thought to herself. "I am home."

won't

Have you heard
about Will Knott?
He is so lazy
he signs his name

work

something you always have to do

Work, work, work! I've never known such a workhorse. Thank goodness she has a workshop! She just sits at that workbench working on her workbook day after day. What a workout! I get all worked up, watching a worker like that!

worm

squiggly   wiggly   wriggly   *jiggly*   ziggly   higgly   piggly   worm   watch   it

Earthworms are animals with soft bodies and no bones that live in moist soil. They have strong muscles with which they can swell up, thin down, stretch out, or pull in. They also have very small bristles all over their bodies. These bristles make it possible for them to crawl. They can move along quite fast when they're in a tunnel. But it's harder for them to move outside where they don't have the sides of the tunnel to cling to.

In loose soil worms make tunnels by pushing the earth aside. In hard-packed soil they form tunnels by swallowing the soil. There are bits of plants and other food mixed in this soil, and the worms digest this food.

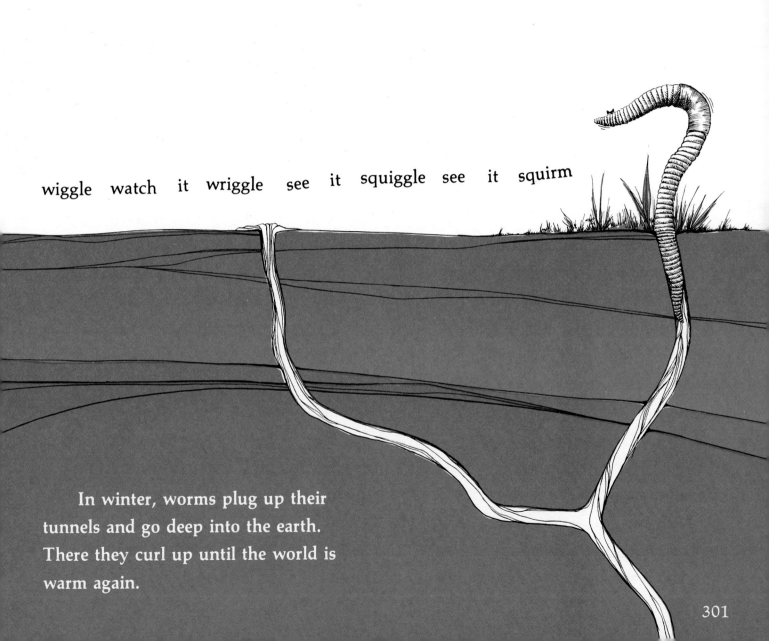

wiggle watch it wriggle see it squiggle see it squirm

In winter, worms plug up their tunnels and go deep into the earth. There they curl up until the world is warm again.

write-up

a story in a newspaper or magazine

"Tonight," Mr. Shuman announced, "it is a great honor to welcome the famous opera star, Madame Maria Melonas."

The audience clapped warmly.

"Thank you," Madame Melonas said. "It is a joy to be here—to sing for you young musicians in the school where I first studied music. Walking upstairs to this room was like walking into my past, when I was a student here at the conservatory. And so tonight," Madame Melonas continued, "I will sing some songs I first learned here."

In the audience, Linda listened to the beautiful voice that filled the room and drifted throughout the building.

Linda was spellbound. The more she listened, the closer she felt to this woman who loved the conservatory as much as she did. To Linda, there could be no better place to study music than in the old mansion with its worn chairs, its frayed carpets, and the musty smell of its rooms. Linda loved to wander through the conservatory from top to bottom—from the dusty attic on the fourth floor down the narrow back staircase to the basement kitchen. Then she would climb back up the stairs again, listening to the whisper of music from all the practice rooms. Walking up and down the backstairs, running her hands along the smooth banisters,

always made Linda feel part of the secret life of the old house.

There was not a sound in the room except for Madame Melonas's voice. Everyone was caught in the spell of its beauty. No one moved.

Then, all at once, the lights went out! The audience gasped.

But Madame only paused for a moment. "It is nothing," she thought. "Just a blown fuse. It will be fixed in a minute. Many worse things have happened in the middle of my performances."

So Madame continued singing in the darkness. The audience, calmed by her voice, listened attentively.

303

All except Linda. She thought she smelled smoke. It was faint at first. But the smell grew stronger. Suddenly she realized what it was. Fire! The beautiful old conservatory was on fire!

"Fire!" someone screamed, just at that moment.

"Don't panic!" cried Mr. Shuman. "Please be calm!"

The room was beginning to fill with smoke. Then someone yelled, "The stairs are on fire! We're trapped! We can't get out!"

"There must be another way out," Madame Melonas said. "What about the back staircase?"

"Yes, yes," cried Mr. Shuman. "But in the dark, I—I can't seem to find it. I can't see anything."

"Here. Over here," called Linda.

"Someone take my hand. Let's all get in a line and hold hands. I can lead the way."

"Quickly. Do as the girl says!" ordered Madame.

The others followed Linda as she led them through the smoky darkness toward the narrow back staircase.

"Watch out to your left," Linda said. "There's an old armchair there.

And to your right, some stacks of music."

"Hurry! Hurry! I can hardly breathe!" someone cried.

"Don't hurry," said Linda. "Just stay calm." Linda led the way down the

stairs. "Carefully now," she said. "There's a loose stair. It's the eighth one down."

"The smoke is getting thicker," someone called. "How much farther?"

"We're almost there," Linda answered. "Don't worry. Turn left at the bottom of the stairs. It's only five or six steps to the basement door."

Then at last, coughing and frightened, they reached the outdoors.

"Thank goodness, we're safe!" cried Mr. Shuman.

A few minutes later, Madame Melonas was talking to a group of reporters. "It's that girl who really saved us," she said. "Without her we'd have been trapped inside."

Early the next morning a messenger arrived at Linda's home. "Flowers for Ms. Linda Braun," he announced when

Linda's mother answered the door. "And here's your morning paper, Ma'am," he added, picking up the paper from the welcome mat.

"Linda!" said Mrs. Braun. "Someone sent you flowers. I wonder who."

"What does the card say, Mama?" Linda asked.

"The card says they're from Madame Melonas," Mrs. Braun replied.

"Mother! Maria Melonas sent *me* flowers?" Linda was so excited she thought she would burst.

"Why not?" asked her mother. "After all, you're quite a celebrity yourself, according to the paper —"

DAILY NEWS
"EXTRA"
BLIND GIRL LEADS
MUSICIANS TO SAFETY

T X H Y I Z S X I Y S Z I X T X Y Z I X T Y I
X S Y A Z L X L Y O Z V X E Y R X Y Z T Z H X
E Y R Z E X W I Z L X L Y B Z E X N Y O Z M
X O Y R Z E X Y Z T X H Y I Z S X I Y S Z T X
H Y E Z E X N Y D Z X Y T Z H X I Y S Z I X S
Y T Z H X E Y V Z E X R Y Y Z L X A Y S Z T X
C Y H Z A X P Y T Z E X R Y O Z F X T Y H Z E
X D Y I Z C X T Y O Z P X E Y D Z I X A X Y Z

X

X
means
kisses

X
means
incorrect

X
means
multiply

X
marks
the
spot

X
is a
choice

X
is the
winner

X?

It seldom starts a word,
A well-known word,
A word you've heard.
X-words do not get used a lot.
I knew one once.
But I forgot.

xylography

the art of printing books or illustrations from wood blocks

Before the days of typewriters and fancy printing presses, copies of books had to be made by hand. This was slow, tiring work. And it was so expensive that only the rich could afford books. Xylography, or wood block printing, changed all this. *Xylo-* comes from an old word that means "wood." And *-graphy* means "writing."

All day every day, summer and winter, spring and fall, I copied books. It was an awful job.

THIS IS *DULL, REALLY DULL.*

Whenever my boss, the Duchess, wanted a copy of a book for someone, I was the one who copied it, word for word, picture for picture.

THREE COPIES OF THIS, JOHANN.

YES.

Three months later, I was still working on the Duchess's copies. I couldn't stand it any longer. There had to be an easier way.

ENOUGH OF THIS— THIS IS CRAZY!

Then I had a brilliant idea.

I picked up a piece of wood and started to work. Carefully I carved out a letter.

I'M SUCH A GENIUS!

I put some ink on the letter I'd carved. Then I pressed the inked letter onto a piece of paper.

OOPS!

It took some thinking to realize that I had to carve the letters *backwards* if I wanted them to come out right.

The best part of my idea was that I could move the letters around to make new words. I didn't have to keep carving more letters.

Then I thought, "Why not do a whole page at once?"

Now the printing press works day after day, summer and winter, fall and spring, making as many copies as I need. I find this very satisfactory.

YELLOW

There is nothing
quite
like the sudden
light
of
forsythia
that
one morning
without warning
explodes
into yellow
and
startles the street
into spring.

313

yesteryear

days long ago

Old Jim Heslop and young Jim Heslop got along just fine, even though old Jim was over ninety and young Jim, his great-grandson, was only ten. Old Jim would sit in his wheelchair in the sun and talk to young Jim. He talked in a loud, deep voice, because he was quite deaf and couldn't hear himself. Young Jim liked his voice. But young Jim never said much. He just listened.

Old Jim liked to talk about the old days. "Those days!" he would say. "Those days weren't like today. There weren't any noisy automobiles then. There were giants on the earth in those days. Why, my grandfather who's buried over in the old town—he was seven feet tall. You can see his tombstone there, like a giant's!"

Old Jim talked to everyone about the old days. The neighbors would listen politely to the old man. Then they would smile at one another and tap their foreheads. They didn't believe him. And even though the Heslop family loved the old man, most of them were too busy to listen to him. Only young Jim listened, and he believed what his great-grandfather said.

"It's true," old Jim said. "It was true, though there's nothing left to prove it. No one believes."

One afternoon, in the middle of a story, old Jim suddenly stopped talking, and he did not start again. Young Jim looked up in surprise. His great-grandfather beckoned him to come close.

"If I speak like this," old Jim said, "can anyone hear but you?"

Young Jim looked around carefully. There were no neighbors in the gardens, and his mother was in the kitchen with the water running. He shook his head.

"What would you say to a trip—a real pleasure trip?" old Jim asked. "Not in one of those noisy automobiles, though."

Young Jim raised his eyebrows.

Old Jim nodded. "Mind you, I know that it's a long push with the wheelchair."

Young Jim nodded and waited.

"It came to me just now in a flash," said old Jim. "We'll go over to the old town. That's where I was born and where my grandfather is buried—he that was seven feet tall. I'll show it to you."

Young Jim said, "When?"

"The sooner the better," said old Jim. "Tomorrow, very early, before there's traffic on the road. Before the others are awake. They might stop us."

Young Jim nodded. If anyone knew, it would spoil the adventure.

"We can leave at sunrise, tomorrow morning," old Jim decided.

The next morning, the summer dawn surprised young Jim. It was so still and gray. He had expected at least reds and yellows in the sky, like a festival. He was surprised, too, at the chill in

the air. He gave his great-grandfather an extra blanket for the wheelchair. They had not planned to have any breakfast at all. But now old Jim saw they would need something to eat later. The most that they dared do was to boil some water and make a thermos of tea. They also put a handful of cookies into a paper bag.

"And," said old Jim in his lowest voice, "we'll take your mother's tape measure." He would not say why.

With old Jim in the wheelchair, and the thermos and cookies and the tape measure on his knees, the two left the house. In all the houses they passed, the curtains were still drawn. None of the neighbors was up. Young Jim pushed the chair along with his heart in his mouth, for the squeak of the wheels sounded very loud in the morning silence.

They left the street and came out onto the main road. There was no traffic at all, until an all-night truck rumbled by. Then nothing again.

They crossed the main road slowly and turned down the road to the old town.

This was a country road, going always deeper into the country. There were wide fields where the grass grew tall, yellowing and drying with the heat of August.

After about an hour, they reached the edge of the old village—a few small cottages and a farmhouse, and the graveyard beyond. There was still no one awake. They heard no sound of life in the old town. Hardly anyone still lived there. They had all moved away.

Young Jim stopped the wheelchair. Old Jim sat silently for a while, remembering.

"I was born in this village," he said to young Jim at last. "And I married your great-grandmother here. She died long before you were born. My mother and father lived here all their lives. And my grandfather before them. Yes, and he's gone, too."

But this reminded old Jim of something. "I'll show you," he said. "Let's go towards the east end of the graveyard."

Young Jim wheeled him along the narrow path that went into the graveyard. Towards the east end old Jim said, "Stop!" He looked around him. "You'll find the tombstone about here. James Heslop his name was—like my name—like yours."

Young Jim began to look. The stones were very old, overgrown and weatherworn. The writing on them was hard to read.

Old Jim saw his great-grandson's difficulty. "Look for a big tombstone—the biggest. Seven feet tall he was, and his tombstone was to match."

"This is the longest tombstone" said young Jim at last. He scraped away the ivy from the head of it. "I can't read the first letters, but here's an S and an L, and this is an O."

"It's Heslop," said old Jim. "It's his. Wheel me closer, boy."

Young Jim brought the chair alongside the tombstone. Old Jim leaned forward with the tape measure he had brought. He placed one end at the head of the tombstone. With difficulty, he stretched the tape measure out full length. It was only a five-foot tape measure, and it did not reach. Young Jim had to measure the rest separately.

"Five feet," he said, "and another two feet nine inches."

"Nearly eight feet," said old Jim, and he lay back in his chair and closed his eyes. "You must tell them all that. Nearly eight feet his tombstone had to be, because in his life he was seven feet tall. There's his tombstone to prove it. Seven feet tall—they were giants in those days."

Then he opened his eyes again and said briskly, "What about the tea?"

Young Jim got out the thermos and the

cookies. They took turns drinking out of the cup top of the thermos, and they ate the cookies. It was still very early, but there was no doubt that the day was going to be another hot one. Bees came out and began to work among the tall weeds. A bird suddenly appeared at the far end of the tombstone, and young Jim threw it some crumbs.

Unexpectedly a car passed. They saw it through the gate in the wall. Then they heard brakes squeal. The car stopped suddenly, and then it backed up until it was by the gate. Then it stopped again. After a moment, two police officers got out and stared at them.

The police opened the gate and began walking up the path. Old Jim and young Jim watched.

The first officer burst out, "Whatever are you doing here, James Heslop, with all your family out looking for you?"

"They're running around the village looking for you," added the second officer.

"Now what were you two up to?" asked the first officer.

Both police waited for an answer to this. Neither old Jim nor young Jim said anything, so the second officer said, "Eh?"

Old Jim smiled and shook his head, and young Jim looked down.

The second officer said suddenly, "The old one's deaf—you remember—the family said so. And they said the child didn't talk much."

"Deaf?" said the first officer. He drew a deep breath into his great chest. In a voice that might have awakened seven-foot James Heslop under his tombstone, the officer shouted, "We've come to take you home in the car, Mr. Heslop."

Old Jim smiled and shook his head.

"Deaf," said the second officer.

Then the two police began to act out what they wanted to do. They pointed to the car. They pretended to drive along. They pointed toward home.

Old Jim clapped his hands and smiled; but he also shook his head.

The police started all over again. But one of them put his hands on the wheelchair as if to push it toward the car.

Then old Jim spoke slowly and quietly. "I don't like cars. I never like to be difficult, but I wouldn't want you to try to get me into a car at my age. My bones are stiff, you know. And then there's my heart."

The police looked at old Jim carefully. He certainly appeared very weak, and he sounded very weak indeed. Yet they had promised the family to find the old man and the boy and to bring them home at once.

"Yet I'd like to be home, too," said old Jim. "It's been a strain—at my age—so early in the morning—to come so far. . . ." He let his voice die away and closed his eyes.

"We should get him home somehow, quickly," said the first officer, looking worried.

In the silence, old Jim suddenly said, "Ah!"

Both officers jumped. Old Jim opened his eyes and said, "You could tow me home."

"Tow you home?" repeated the police officers.

"Fasten my wheelchair to the back of your car with a rope," old Jim explained.

The officers looked at each other. They had never heard of such a thing being done.

"It'd be a question for the Traffic Department, probably," said the first officer.

"There'd be rules and regulations about it," said the second.

"For instance, he'd have to have his own license plate," said the first.

"Yes, he'd have to be called a trailer," said the second.

Old Jim did not hear, but he could see they weren't doing anything. He became impatient.

"If you don't have a rope," old Jim said

sharply, "handcuffs would do. You could hand-cuff the wheelchair to the back of the car. Surely you have handcuffs in a police car."

"But you'd be a trailer!" shouted the first officer.

"I'd be *what?*" asked old Jim. It was not clear whether he had not heard or could not believe what he had heard.

The first officer shook his head. "It wouldn't be safe, anyway," he said.

"Unless, of course," said the second officer, "we drove very slowly and carefully." He was beginning to like the idea.

"That's possible," the first officer agreed. "But, however you look at it, he'd be a trailer. I don't think it would be legal."

At this point young Jim surprised them by speaking. "But nobody would see."

That was quite true. It was still so early that nobody was on the roads. On the other hand, the later it got, the greater the chance of meeting someone. If they were to act at all, they must act quickly.

The second officer persuaded the first. It turned out that they always carried a good tow rope in the car. They fastened the front of the wheelchair—with old Jim still in it—to the back of the police car. Young Jim got into the back seat of the car. One officer sat with him, and the other drove.

They went very slowly for a car, but much more quickly than a wheelchair could ever have been pushed. From the beginning to the end of the journey, young Jim and the officer with him kept watch through the rear window. Young Jim pressed his nose against the glass. He was worried.

At first old Jim looked worried, too. But the faster he went, the happier he seemed to become. His white hair streamed in the wind. He began to signal to the two in the back seat for the car to go

faster still. They did not pass his message on to the driver. Already the wheelchair was traveling at a speed no one had ever dreamed of before.

Old Jim began to sing, though the people in the car couldn't hear him. They could see his lips moving as he sang all the way home.

They turned into the Heslop's street, and there was the family, waiting.

Young Jim got out of the car quickly and said, "Mom, I've come all the way from the old town in a police car!"

After breakfast, old Jim said that he was not really tired after all. He said he would like to sit out in the shade, in his usual chair, at the front of the house. Young Jim made him comfortable there.

"Yes," said the old man, "those days. . . ." He laughed to himself. "But what my grandfather would have said to see me rolling along this morning! The best of both worlds—that's what I've had!"

yo-yo

How to Make a Yo-Yo in Eight Easy Steps

1. Buy two mushrooms that are exactly the same size. (If you use mushrooms that are different sizes, your yo-yo will wobble.)

2. Make sure that the stems of the mushrooms are thin but strong. (If they're not strong enough, the yo-yo will break in half the first time you try it out.)

3. Paint the two mushrooms with nice colors and designs. (A coat of paint will protect your yo-yo and make it last longer, too.)

4. After the paint has dried, take your mushrooms and cut the stems short. (If the stems are too long, the yo-yo will droop. Now go wash your hands if you didn't wait for the paint to dry.)

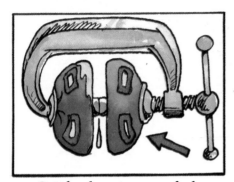

5. Stick the stems of the two mushrooms together firmly. (If you don't use enough glue, the two halves of the yo-yo will fly apart at the first flick of the wrist.)

6. Tie a string around the mushroom stems. (The string should be just long enough to reach from your hand to the ground.)

7. Get a magician to turn the mushrooms into wood for you. (Just the mushrooms—not the string.)

8. Thank the magician. (It's hard work being a magician.)

329

zoology

Zoology is the study of animals. Zoologists are the people who study animals.

People have been collecting and observing animals for thousands of years. More than a million different kinds of animals have been found. And new kinds of animals are discovered as more and more of the world is explored. In order to keep track of all these different kinds of animals, scientists found that they needed a system for naming animals.

At first, when people discovered a new kind of animal, they named it in whatever language they happened to speak. People who spoke different languages naturally gave different names to what was really the same kind of animal. People who spoke Spanish might call an animal a *puma*. But people who spoke Portuguese called the same

animal a *cuguardo*. And people who spoke English called it a mountain lion or a catamount or a panther. This could be very confusing. So it was important to find names that all zoologists could agree on.

More than two hundred years ago, scientists decided to use just one language for naming animals. They chose Latin as the language because most scientists then could read it and write it, even though nobody actually spoke Latin anymore.

Each different kind of animal is given two Latin names, a general one and a specific one. The general name is like a person's last name and tells what "family" an animal belongs to. The

specific name is like a person's first name and tells which specific member of that "family" it is.

The general name comes first and begins with a capital letter. The specific name comes second and begins with a lower-case letter. For example, the Latin name for lion is *Panthera leo*; the name for tiger is *Panthera tigris*; and a leopard is a *Panthera pardus*. This shows that lions, tigers, and leopards all belong to the same general "family" of large cats called *Panthera*. But they are all different members of that "family."

Panthera tigris

Panthera leo

Panthera pardus

zyzzyva

a tropical insect that eats plants

A zyzzyva knows all that there is
from A to Z
and Z to A
because that's what a zyzzyva's business is.

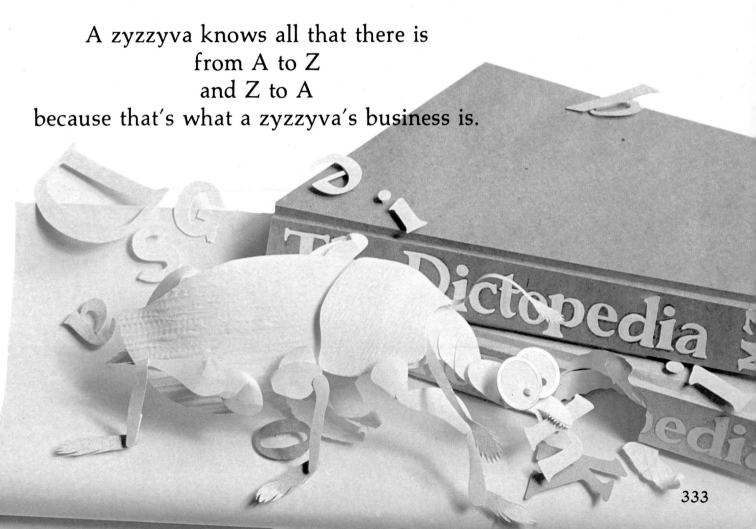

answer page

palindrome

A palindrome is a word, phrase, or sentence that says the same thing, whether you read it forwards or backwards.

rectangle

McJangular is made of 15 rectangles: 2 feet, 2 legs, 2 arms, 1 finger, 1 mouth, 3 teeth, 2 eyes, 1 head, 1 body.

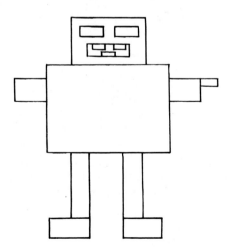

T

The two riders were on a tandem (a bicycle built for two).

unmarked

Put the signpost back in the hole with the name of the town you just left pointing back to the road you just walked on. Now all the other signs will point in the correct directions, and you can tell which road goes to Mudville.

Acknowledgments

(continued from page 3)

Copyright © 1972 by Judy Blume. Reprinted by permission of the publishers, E. P. Dutton. Page 270, adapted from "A Chimp in the Garden of Eden" from *Congo Kitabu* by Jean-Pierre Hallet. Copyright © 1965 by Jean-Pierre Hallet. Page 277, "74th Street" (retitled "Victory") from *The Malibu and Other Poems* by Myra Cohn Livingston (A Margaret K. McElderry Book). Copyright © 1972 by Myra Cohn Livingston. Used by permission of Atheneum Publishers.

W page 279 (left), L. Rosal. Page 279 (right), "The Wapiti" from *Verses From 1929 On* by Ogden Nash, by permission of Little, Brown and Co. Copyright © 1933 by Ogden Nash. Page 280, © Tsá' Ászi', Pine Hill CPO Box 12, Ramah, New Mexico 87321. Ramah Navajo School Board, Inc. Page 284, A. Humez. Page 285, "Wish," Shirleyann Costigan. Page 299 (left), courtesy of *Boys' Life Magazine*. Page 299 (right), T. Lapham. Page 300 (poem), "Worm" from *A Little Book of Little Beasts*. Copyright © 1973 by Mary Ann Hoberman. Reprinted by permission of Simon & Schuster, a Division of Gulf & Western Corporation. Page 300 (text), A. Humez. Page 302, "Write-up," L. Rosal.

XYZ page 307, T. Lapham. Page 308, "X," from *Play on Words* by Alice and Martin Provensen. Copyright © 1972 by Alice and Martin Provensen. Reprinted by permission of Random House, Inc. Page 309, "X?" from *Nuts to You and Nuts to Me* by Mary Ann Hoberman. Copyright © 1974 by Mary Ann Hoberman. Reprinted by permission of Alfred A. Knopf, Inc. Page 310, T. Lapham and A. Humez. Page 313, "Forsythia Bush," text copyright © 1969 by Lilian Moore. From *I Thought I Heard the City.* Used by permission of Atheneum Publishers. Page 314, adaptation of "Still Jim and Silent Jim" © 1959 by Philippa Pearce. From the book *What the Neighbors Did and Other Stories* by Philippa Pearce. Reprinted by permission of Thomas Y. Crowell Company and Penguin Books Ltd. Page 328, A. Humez. Page 330, A. Humez. Page 333, T. Lapham.

The concept of *The Dictopedia* was suggested by Ellen Radtke.

Artist credits

Elizabeth A. Barry, designer

M pages 6-11, from *Colleen Moore's Dollhouse* by Colleen Moore. ICC copyright © 1971. Reprinted by permission of Doubleday & Company, Inc. The dollhouse is located at the Museum of Science and Industry in Chicago; pages 12-15, Tony Chen; pages 16-27, Kinuko Craft; pages 28-29, Jon McIntosh; page 30, Nancy Lawton; pages 32-33, Charles Molina; page 34, Keith Gunnar, Bruce Coleman, Inc.

N pages 36-37, Tom Cooke; page 38, Joel Schick; pages 39-43, Arvis Stewart; page 44, Meredith Lightbown; pages 45-46, Kenneth Long-

Trelawney N. Goodell, art editor

temps; pages 47-50, Arvis Stewart; page 51, Jon Goodell; pages 52-54, Bob Barner; pages 55-59, Arvis Stewart.

O pages 62-77, Friso Henstra; pages 78-79, Donald Carrick; page 80, Bob Barner; pages 81-88, Salvatore Catalano; pages 88-89, The Norton Simon Foundation, Los Angeles; page 90 (left), Bob Barner; page 90 (right), Ingrid Koepcke.

P page 91, Diedra Delano Stead; page 92, Martucci Studio; pages 93-95,

Ruth Brunner-Strosser; pages 96-99, John Brosnan's *Movie Magic*; page 99 (right), from *Talking Words*, by Ashok Davar, copyright © 1969 by Ashok Davar. Reprinted by permission of The Bobbs-Merrill Company, Inc.; pages 100-101, Mordicai Gerstein; pages 102-104, Les Morrill; pages 105-112, Jerry Pinkney; pages 113-116, Vermont Hand Carved Signs, Diedra Delano Stead (photographs).

Q pages 118-122, Roberto Innocenti; page 123, Ronald LeHew; page 124, Naiad Einsel; page 125, illustration by Mercer Mayer is reprinted from *A Poison Tree* by permission of Charles Scribner's Sons. Copyright © 1977 Mercer Mayer; page 126, British Tourist Authority; page 127, London Daily Mail; page 128, Boston Academy of Applied Sciences, Photo Trends; page 129 (top), Boston Academy of Applied Sciences, Photo Trends; page 129 (bottom), Sue B. Thompson; page 130 (left), Boston Academy of Applied Sciences, Photo Trends; page 130 (middle and right), Sue B. Thompson; pages 132-133, Alice deKok; pages 134-141, David Chestnutt.

R pages 143-149, Richard Walz; page 150, Jane Dyer; page 151 (right), Martucci Studio; pages 152-158, John Gamache; page 159, Diedra Delano Stead; pages 160-161, William Shirley; pages 162-167, Annette Thompson/womenSports; page 167 (right), Terri Huizinga.

S pages 168-170, Trevor Smith; pages 171-175, Lois Ireland; page 176 (left), Vera Gerken Kurtz; page 176 (right), Bruce Raskin, *Learning Magazine*; page 177, Jan Naimo; pages 178-183, Dora Leder; page 184, Diedra Delano Stead; page 184 (bottom), The Bettman Archive Inc.; page 185, Lucinda McQueen; pages 186-192, John E. Johnson. Copyright © 1967 by Oliver G. Selfridge and John E. Johnson. Reprinted by permission of Houghton Mifflin Company; page 193, National Solar Heating and Cooling Information Center; pages 194-195, Norris Strawbridge.

T page 196, Bob Barner; page 197, Janet Mager; pages 198-199, photographs courtesy of Champion Papers *Imagination* XVI — Brazil; pages 200-202, Amy Myers; page 203, David McPhail; page 204, Jack Stokes; page 205-209, Robert Conrad; page 210 (top), Bob Barner; page 210 (bottom), Trevor Smith; pages 211-223, John Burgoyne.

U page 224, Arlene Dubanovich; page 225, Leslie Richmond; pages 226-234, Jennie Williams; page 235 (left), Bob Barner; page 235 (right), Bernice Myers; pages 236-239, Shelley Freshman; page 242 (top and bottom right), Murphy's Photo Supplies; page 242 (bottom left), North Carolina Department of Commerce; page 243 (top left and center), King, Florida Department of Commerce; page 243 (top right) H. Armstrong Roberts; page 243 (bottom left), Columbia College Photo Project; page 244, Jan Palmer; pages 245-249, John Freas; pages 250-251, Ron Barrett.

V page 252, Alan Magee; page 253, Marc Brown; pages 254-256, Jan Trier; pages 257-259, Victoria Chess; pages 260-262, Ruth Brunner-Strosser; page 263, Diedra Delano Stead; pages 264-269, John Wallner; pages 270-276, Hal Frenck; page 277, Eric A. Roth.

W page 279 (left), Martucci Studio; page 279 (right) Joanne Fabris; pages 280-283, John Swatsley; page 284 (top), W.B. Finch, Stock, Boston, Inc.; page 284 (left), Mike Mazzaschi, Stock, Boston, Inc.; page 284 (right), Mary I. Cuffe, *Historic Preservation*; pages 285-298, Judy Love; page 299 (left), Bob Dole; page 299 (right), Ed Renfro; pages 300-301, copyright © 1973 by Peter Parnall. Reprinted by permission of Simon & Schuster, a Division of Gulf & Western Corporation; pages 302-306, David Chestnutt.

XYZ pages 308-309, Alice and Martin Provensen. Copyright © 1972 by Alice and Martin Provensen. Reprinted by permission of Random House, Inc.; pages 310-312, Lydia Dabcovich; page 313, Eric A. Roth; pages 314-327, Terry Pascoe; pages 328-329, Jon McIntosh; pages 330-332, Jean Helmer; page 333, Elissa Della-Piana, Diedra Delano Stead (photograph).

Our thanks to Bill Wall for *pancakes, relish, wallpaper*.
Mechanical art, Ann Lampton Curtis, Joe Durkin.